Math Matters:
The Links Between High School Curriculum, College Graduation, and Earnings

• • •

Heather Rose
Julian R. Betts

2001

PUBLIC POLICY INSTITUTE OF CALIFORNIA

Library of Congress Cataloging-in-Publication Data
Rose, Heather, 1971–
    Math matters : the links between high school curriculum, college
graduation, and earnings / Heather Rose, Julian R. Betts.
       p. cm.
    Includes bibliographical references.
    ISBN 1-58213-029-9
       1. Mathematics—Study and teaching (Secondary)—United
States. 2. Education—Economic aspects—United States.
3. Academic achievement—United States. 4. Wages—Effect of
education on—United States.   I. Betts, Julian R..   II. Title.

QA13 .R64 2001
510'.71'273—dc21   2001019915

Research publications reflect the views of the authors and do not
necessarily reflect the views of the staff, officers, or Board of
Directors of the Public Policy Institute of California.

Foreword

In an effort to address the poor performance of students graduating from California schools, the public policy debate has focused on more spending, smaller class sizes, teacher hiring, and a more equitable allocation of resources. For some reason, it seems that school curriculum has received less attention. Yet, as important as other concerns are, student outcomes will always be related to the type and quality of the available curriculum. In this study, Heather Rose and Julian Betts focus on the relationship between the math courses students take in high school, whether they graduate from college, and their earnings in the labor force 10 years after graduating from high school.

The authors' conclusions are encouraging. Math curriculum—especially advanced courses such as algebra and geometry—has a positive effect on college graduation and on earnings later in life. Although these are findings that might seem obvious to some, and explained by privileged backgrounds for others, this study finds that the effect of math courses on later earnings does not appear to vary much with respect to student or school characteristics and that a rigorous math curriculum at any school can benefit students of any type. Another important finding of this study is that not all math courses are equal. To quote the authors, "It is not simply the number of math courses that matters; what matters more is the extent to which students take more demanding courses such as algebra and geometry."

The findings of this study underscore the importance of local school districts' meeting the challenge by recruiting qualified teachers trained in mathematics and by offering all students the opportunity to take a full range of advanced math courses in high school. The authors note that schools should not suddenly *require* that all students take advanced math courses, but they should encourage and prepare them to do so.

This study is one of a series of projects under way at PPIC on education policy for the state of California. Future reports will include contributions to the new master plan for California's system of public education; an analysis of student achievement in San Diego; an examination of the relationship between teacher quality and the achievement of minority and low-income students; and a study to determine how the educational needs of new immigrants might be better met. *Math Matters* is the first step in our effort to look carefully at what schools are offering to students and how those offerings affect their long-term economic and social well-being.

David W. Lyon
President and CEO
Public Policy Institute of California

Summary

A recurrent concern in the debate over education reform is that schools are not doing a good job in preparing students, especially minority and disadvantaged students, to excel in school and to be successful in the labor market. This concern has led to a variety of government responses over the years, some of which have focused on curriculum. In 1983, the National Commission on Excellence in Education recommended a more rigorous high school curriculum. It outlined a "New Basics" curriculum that included, among other things, four years of English and three years of math. Many states have since upgraded their graduation requirements. California, which has traditionally granted districts some autonomy in setting curriculum, has adopted statewide content standards in a number of subjects over the last few years. Most recently, on September 30, 2000, California Governor Gray Davis approved a bill making algebra a requirement for high school graduation.

Considerable evidence suggests that differences in years of schooling explain a large portion of the income gap in the nation and in California. Many have inferred that the growing income gap can be narrowed by better educating people at the lower end of the income distribution, especially minority students.

It stands to reason that it is not just years of education, but the type of education—the courses taken during school—that affects the earnings of high school students years later. There is some limited evidence that students who take more math in high school are more likely to pursue postsecondary education and to have higher earnings in the future. However, it has not been established how strong these relationships are, for what groups they exist, and what else might explain the apparent effect of curriculum on postsecondary education and future earnings.

Despite the belief that an enhanced curriculum is one way to improve students' college attendance rates and earnings, the few studies that do include curriculum in estimates of these long-run student outcomes generally find minimal effects. The notion that the actual courses that students take in high school do not matter raises serious questions about the effectiveness of the American public school system's curriculum. Therefore, it is essential to investigate further.

The purpose of this report is to answer a series of broad questions:

1. What kind of math courses do which students take? Is there a link between the type of math courses that students take, the probability that students earn a college degree, and their future earnings?

2. If there is a link, does it reflect the effect that math courses have on students' productivity and therefore earnings, or does it merely reflect other underlying factors, such as a student's ability and motivation? (These other factors may determine both the level of math courses that a student takes and his or her future earnings.)

3. What are the policy implications of the study's findings?

This report focuses on the relationship between mathematics curriculum and earnings because a student's earnings are arguably the ultimate measure of how well schools prepare students for the labor market, and because recent evidence indicates that math achievement is more strongly correlated with labor market success than other measures of student achievement. Despite the importance of math courses, we extend the analysis to other subjects as well.

From a policy perspective, a clear understanding of the effects of math courses is extremely important. This is especially true for California where, after considerable debate, Governor Gray Davis and the State Board of Education have decided to include algebra in high school graduation requirements and a new high school "exit" exam. Understanding the economic value of such a course would be useful in justifying or modifying such policies.

There are also more general reasons why it is important to understand the effects of mathematics curriculum. First, to intervene in education effectively, we must understand whether students' destinies have been determined by the time they reach high school or whether a rigorous high school curriculum can alter students' paths. If it turns out that high school has little influence over student outcomes, intervention is necessary at an earlier stage. On the other hand, if high school curriculum does affect educational and labor market outcomes, policies aimed at encouraging students to take a more advanced curriculum may be a way of increasing the flow into college and increasing student earnings later in life.

Second, with the recent elimination of affirmative action programs in California and some other states, there is fear that minority access to postsecondary education has suffered. As the returns to a college education continue to rise, such limited access would have severe implications for income equality between different ethnic groups. In light of the disappearance of race-based admissions policies, encouraging minority students to take more math, and improving their educational foundations so that they can do so, may help to increase their enrollment in college.

Finally, if we can establish that a more rigorous curriculum indeed affects the probability of going on to college and having higher future earnings, there will be many implications for how school resources are allocated. Perhaps more money should be spent on improving curriculum options, as opposed to spending designed to reduce class sizes. In sum, a clear understanding of the effects of curriculum and of possible variations in these effects related to student and school characteristics will guide policymakers about how best to equip students with the skills and education necessary to be successful once they leave school.

To answer the questions set forth in this report, we use the longitudinal data collected in the High School and Beyond survey of a representative national sample of students who were in grade 10 in 1980. This survey includes detailed data from the students' high school transcripts, information about the highest educational degree the student attained, and information about earnings nearly 10 years after students should have graduated from high school. The rich demographic data, as well as information about the student's family and high school, permit us to account for many noncurriculum factors that may also be related to college graduation and earnings. Because the survey data do not contain

enough California students to estimate separate statistical models for
California, most of the analysis proceeds at the national level.
Nonetheless, we have enough California data to perform some checks
that indicate that the predictions from the national models apply to
California.

Mathematics Course-Taking Behavior of the 1982 Senior High School Class

There was a great deal of variation in the course-taking behavior of
students in the early 1980s. Figure S.1 shows the proportion of students
who completed at least one semester of the given level of mathematics
course, as their highest course, by the time they graduated (or dropped
out) from high school. A staggering 26 percent of students completed

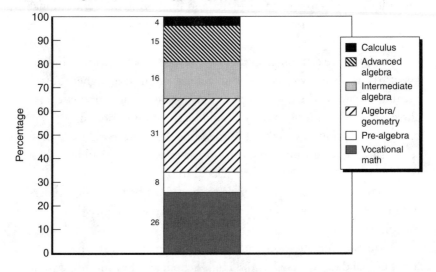

SOURCE: HSB sophomore cohort.

NOTES: Sample includes public school students who have completed at least
one semester in at least one math course and are not missing any pertinent math
transcript data. The highest math course is considered to be that in which the
student completed at least one semester. The number of observations included is
10,073. The frequencies are weighted by the HSB transcript weight. Unweighted,
the values are 26 percent, 9 percent, 30 percent, 16 percent, 16 percent, and
4 percent, respectively.

Figure S.1—Highest Math Course Taken

only vocational math courses and nothing more before leaving high school.[1] Another 8 percent stopped taking math courses after completing pre-algebra. Thirty-one percent took at least an algebra or geometry course, but nothing beyond; and a roughly equal percentage took an even more advanced math course. Only 4 percent of students completed a calculus course.[2]

This variation in course-taking had long-term implications for the welfare of these students. Figures S.2 and S.3 reveal that the point where students ended their math taking is related to how much education these

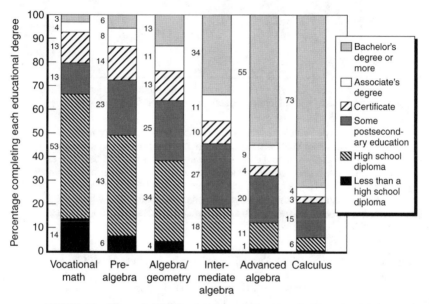

NOTES: See Figure 2.1 for the data source, sample criteria, and weighting. The sample size is only 8,850 because of missing data on educational attainment.

Figure S.2—Highest Degree Earned by 1992 Related to Highest Math Course Taken in High School

---

[1]Vocational math courses include courses described as vocational math, general math, basic math, consumer math, and math review.

[2]We consider the highest course to be the highest-level course in which the student completed at least one semester. However, in our more detailed models of earnings, we consider a course to be a year-long course.

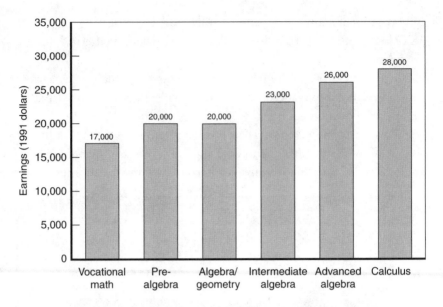

NOTES: The sample includes public school students who have completed at least one semester in at least one math course, are not missing any pertinent math transcript data, have annual earnings between $2,000 and $75,000, and are not enrolled in any postsecondary education program. The number of observations included is 5,891. The medians are weighted by the HSB fourth follow-up weights. In 1999 dollars, the above earnings are vocational math, $20,794; pre-algebra, $24,464; algebra/geometry, $28,134; advanced algebra, $31,803; and calculus, $34,250.

Figure S.3—Median 1991 Annual Earnings, by Highest Math Course Taken

students obtained overall and to how much they eventually earned. Students who took more-advanced math courses during high school tended to obtain markedly higher levels of education, and a decade after graduation, they earned significantly more than those who took only lower-level courses.

Given the stark differences in long-term outcomes for students, the fact that a high percentage completed only vocational math is troubling. Even more troublesome is the ethnic composition of these students. Black and Hispanic students were about twice as likely as whites and three times as likely as Asians to cease their math career at this low level. Similarly, students of extremely low-income families were much less likely to take any academic math courses. Figures S.4 and S.5 show the

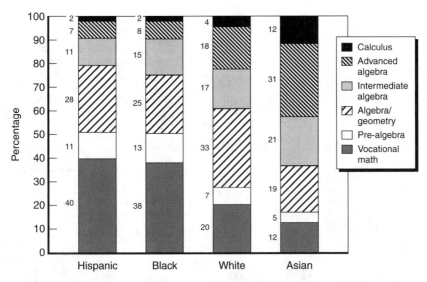

NOTES: See Figure 2.1 for the data source, sample criteria, weighting, and sample size. When these course completion rates are computed without weights, they are broadly similar to the ones above. The biggest difference is in the number of Hispanic and black students who take vocational math. In these two cases, the unweighted values are 5 percentage points lower than the weighted case, with the slack being taken up in the higher-level courses. The sample sizes for the ethnic groups are 2,221, 1,320, 5,855, and 345 for Hispanic, black, white, and Asian, respectively.

Figure S.4—Highest Math Course Taken, by Ethnicity

math courses taken by each ethnic group and parental income group. The minority students and students from low-income families who disproportionately stopped taking math at early stages also tended to be the students who did not progress very far through the school system and who tended to be at the low end of the income distribution later on in life.

Although the level of math course a student takes is correlated with college graduation rates and earnings, the correlations do not necessarily imply causation. There may be some underlying student characteristic that causes students to take a more rigorous curriculum and earn higher wages in the future. Nonetheless, the correlations do raise a red flag indicating the need for more in-depth analysis. When we conducted this analysis and estimated the effect that math courses have on our two

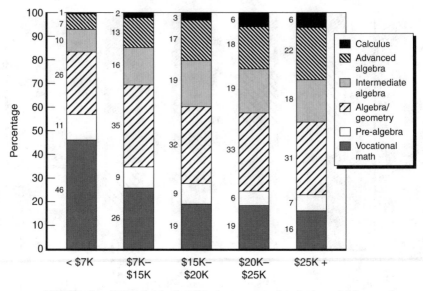

NOTES: See Figure 2.1 for the data source, sample criteria, weighting, and sample size. The sample sizes for the income groups are 916, 2,833, 1,751, 1,503, and 2,258, respectively, from the lowest to the highest income category. The income categories are in 1980 dollars. The 1999 dollar equivalents are roughly double the 1980 values.

Figure S.5—Highest Math Course Taken, by Parental Income

outcomes of interest (college graduation and earnings), we took into account as many of these underlying factors as we could to net out the true curriculum effects. Figure S.6 provides a sketch of the relationship that we model in this report. The student's demographic characteristics include ethnicity and gender; family background characteristics include parental education and income; and high school inputs and resources include things such as school size, teacher's education level, and the percentage of students at the school who are disadvantaged. We expect all of these factors to influence both the type of math courses students take and their educational attainment and earnings. The effect that math courses have on earnings operates through two channels, as shown in the figure: through some cognitive effect that makes students more productive and through an educational attainment effect that makes

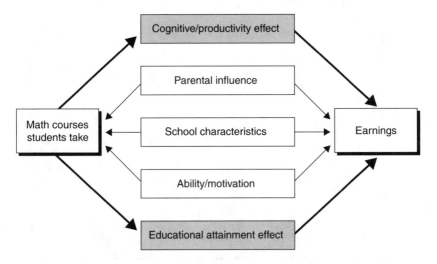

Figure S.6—The Pathways Through Which Curriculum Affects Earnings
(and potentially confounding factors)

students more likely to pursue higher education. We estimated these two pieces of the overall earnings effect.

The Effects of Math Courses on the Likelihood of College Graduation

A large part of a math course's effect on earnings can be explained by its effect on the student's ultimate level of education. Different types of mathematics courses have different effects on the predicted probability of graduating from college, even after controlling for the student's demographic traits, family and school characteristics, and measures of ability. For example, as Figure S.7 shows, whereas the overall probability that an average student[3] whose highest math course is algebra/geometry will graduate is almost 15 percent, the probability that a student who takes intermediate algebra will graduate is nearly 27 percent. And an average student who takes advanced algebra is over 10 percentage points

[3]An average student is considered to be a student with the mean values for all of the explanatory factors in the graduation model.

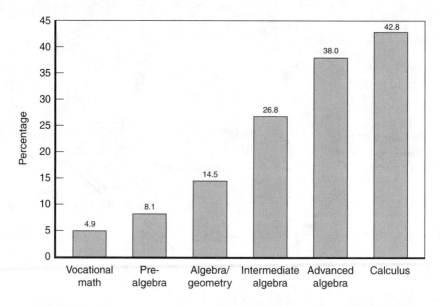

NOTES: When estimating the math effects, we control for the student's demographic, family, and school characteristics as well as the student's ability as measured by his or her math GPA and math test score. The highest completed math course is the highest-level course in which the student completed at least one semester.

Figure S.7—Predicted Percentage of Students Graduating from College Given Their Highest Completed Math Course

more likely to graduate from college than is a student who completes only intermediate algebra.[4]

The Effects of Math Courses on Earnings

The effect that an additional mathematics course has on earnings is quite strong, and it varies by the level of the mathematics course even after accounting for the student's demographic traits, family background characteristics, and high school inputs and resources. As shown in Figure S.8, an additional algebra or geometry course is associated with over 6

---

[4]The highest math course is the highest-level math course in which the student completed at least one semester.

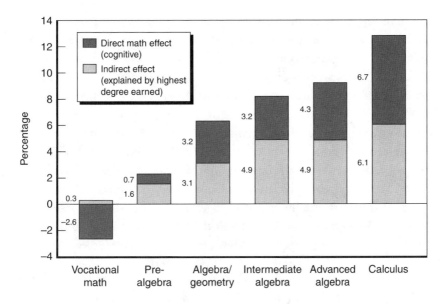

NOTES: When estimating the math effects, we control for the student's demographic, family, and school characteristics. An additional math course refers to an additional year-long course.

Figure S.8—Predicted Percentage Increase in Earnings Resulting from an Additional Math Course (direct and indirect effects)

percent higher earnings, holding all other factors constant.[5] The predicted effect of an additional calculus course is double that. The vocational math effect is somewhat more complicated to interpret. It has a negative sign, implying that students who take one more vocational math course than the average student does have lower earnings than the average student.

The student's ultimate level of educational attainment accounts for half of the academic math course effects, indicating that a large part of the pathway through which mathematics may affect earnings is by increasing the likelihood that students will seek higher education. Figure S.8 shows the predicted percentage difference in earnings resulting from

[5]In this section, we consider a course to last a year. In other words, we report the predicted effects of an additional 1.0 Carnegie unit (or credit) in the course.

an additional math course as well as the portion of that math effect that can be explained by the ultimate level of education that a student obtains. The light and dark bars in the figure show how the total effect of a math class can be broken down into the direct cognitive effect on earnings and the indirect effect on earnings that works by enabling the student to obtain more education. For instance, consider two students who have similar background characteristics and the same ultimate level of education. If one student takes an algebra/geometry course in high school and the other takes, in addition to algebra/geometry, intermediate and advanced algebra, the latter student is predicted to earn 7.5 percent more than the former (intermediate algebra is predicted to increase earnings 3.2 percent and advanced algebra is predicted to increase earnings another 4.3 percent). These are the *direct effects* on earnings. But in addition, as shown by the lighter bars in the figure, the student who takes the additional two courses is also likely to obtain more postsecondary education, boosting his or her earnings another 9.8 percent (4.9 percent for each class). The total combined effect is a predicted earnings gain of 17.3 percent. This is the sum of the two effects of curriculum outlined in Figure S.6, the direct cognitive and the indirect educational attainment effects.

As the diagram in Figure S.6 shows, in addition to accounting for demographic, family, and school characteristics, it is also important to account for other factors, including the student's ability and motivation, to net out the true cognitive/productivity math effects. Accounting for such factors using the students' mathematics grade point average (GPA) explains a portion of the cognitive math effect on earnings.[6] Figure S.9 shows the *direct* math effects that include ability effects and the direct math effects net of ability effects. Controlling for ability and motivation diminishes the *direct* effect of mathematics, and it appears to explain a larger portion of the more advanced math course effects (intermediate algebra and higher) than it does of the algebra/geometry and vocational effects. Nonetheless, once we account for ability, the courses at or above

---

[6]In the main text and Appendix C of this report, we present results from other ways of controlling for ability and motivation. Regardless of the exact control, the tenor of the results does not change.

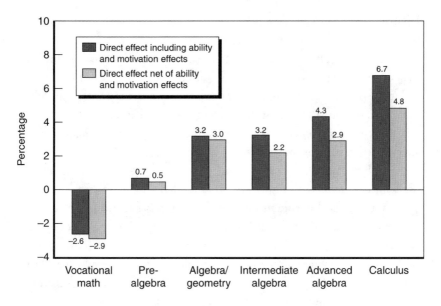

NOTES: When estimating the math effects, we control for the student's demographic, family, and school characteristics. To estimate the effects net of ability and motivation, we also control for the student's math GPA. An additional math course refers to an additional year-long course.

Figure S.9—Predicted Percentage Increase in Earnings Resulting from an Additional Math Course (direct effects with and without ability and motivation)

the algebra level are still associated with much higher earnings than are vocational math and pre-algebra courses. The magnitude of the academic math course effects still differs depending on the course, i.e., calculus has a stronger effect than algebra, but the differences are not as great once we account for ability.

We also examined whether the effect of curriculum on earnings depended significantly on certain characteristics of the schools that students attend, or on the demographic characteristics of the students themselves. This is a crucial concern for policymakers, who will want to know whether, for instance, the math curriculum offered at affluent schools with many resources and largely upper-income white students will prove as effective in a different school and socioeconomic environment. Similarly, we need to know whether curriculum works differently among men and women.

Math curriculum is predicted to affect earnings significantly for both men and women. However, for men, unlike women, most of the influence of curriculum appears to work through the effect that high school math courses have on the student's ultimate level of educational attainment. For women, the direct cognitive/productivity effect is stronger than it is for men.

Similarly, we sought to examine whether the effect of math courses on earnings varied with respect to other student characteristics, characteristics of the student body at the high school, and measures of school resources. We did not find strong evidence that the effect of curriculum changed with respect to any of these variables. If anything, we found weak evidence that taking more math courses might have larger beneficial effects for students from relatively disadvantaged backgrounds. However, we do not find our evidence in this regard decisive.

Finally, although these results are estimated using national data, statistical tests suggest that they apply to California students as well.

The Effects of Math Courses on the Earnings Gap

Considering the important role that math curriculum plays in predicting earnings, it is important to ask a follow-up question: Can math explain the earnings gap between students of different ethnicity or the gap between students from different socioeconomic backgrounds? For the 1980 sophomore cohort, the gap in 1991 earnings between white and black and between white and Hispanic students can be almost entirely explained by demographic, family, and school characteristics, with parental income levels and parental education levels playing a substantial explanatory role.

In turn, curriculum does explain about one-quarter of the earnings gap between the students from the lowest-income families and students from middle-income families. Even more striking, it explains almost the entire gap between the students from the next-to-lowest parental income category and students from middle-income families. So, it appears that curriculum directly explains a portion of the earnings gap based on students' family income level when they are in high school. And, because

Hispanic and black students tend to be overrepresented in the lowest two income groups (in other words, ethnicity and family income level are quite related for these student groups), curriculum indirectly explains part of the ethnic earnings gap as well.

Conclusions

The main message of this report is that math matters. For the 1980 cohort of high school sophomores, math curriculum is strongly related to student outcomes more than 10 years later. Math curriculum has a strong effect on the probability of graduating from college. High school math courses also appear to influence earnings. Roughly half of the predicted effect of math courses on earnings works indirectly through enabling students to obtain more postsecondary education, and the other half appears to work through a direct effect on earnings, independent of how much education the student ultimately obtains.

Although this report focuses on math, we devote a section to the effects of courses in other academic subjects as well. As with math, different types of courses within a certain subject area affect earnings differently. Taking an above-level English course is predicted to increase earnings by more than taking average-level English courses. More interesting, math courses still seem to matter once we account for the courses a student takes in other subjects. It appears that taking an advanced-level English course increases earnings by more than an additional course in algebra/geometry, or intermediate algebra, but by less than the more advanced math courses do. However, all of the math courses at or above the algebra/geometry level are predicted to increase earnings by more than an average-level English course.

A notable finding of the report for policymakers is that the observed correlation between math courses and earnings appears to be at least partly causal. That is, in spite of our extensive efforts to take into account confounding factors, including the student's innate ability and motivation, the relationship between curriculum and earnings still appears strong. Perhaps the most important message of this report is that not all math courses are equal. More-advanced math courses have a much larger effect on college graduation rates and earnings than do less-advanced courses. The biggest difference is between courses at or above the algebra/geometry level and courses below the algebra/geometry level. This finding implies that all students should have access to the full range of demanding math courses and that they should be strongly encouraged, motivated, and prepared to take them. Again, it is not simply the number of math courses that matters; what matters more is the extent to which students take the more demanding courses, such as algebra/geometry.

Although the results of this inquiry show that students who take more-advanced math courses benefit from them, it is important to note one limitation of this finding. These results do not speak to the consequences of policies requiring that all students take a specific math course for graduation. Policies that force certain math courses on students could have negative consequences, such as high student dropout rates and a watering down of the work required to complete those courses. This report does not analyze such consequences. Any policymakers considering sweeping curriculum reform would be well advised to initiate small-scale demonstrations of the reforms to test for such negative side-effects before implementing them widely.

We conclude by noting that in California, perhaps even more so than in other states, public attention continues to focus on such issues as class size, school spending, and teacher quality. Although such public attention is welcome, this report shows that it is crucial to remember that quite independent of the level of resources at a given school, curriculum appears to matter tremendously for long-term student outcomes. Put differently, we must not lose focus on the heart of the matter: what students actually learn in school.

Contents

Figures

Tables

Acknowledgments

Several people helped us throughout this research project. We thank Paul Hill, Richard Murnane, Kim Rueben, and Michael Shires for their valuable reviews of an earlier draft. We also appreciate the insightful comments from Mark Appelbaum, Bud Mehan, Valerie Ramey, and Steven Raphael during early presentations of this work. Gary Bjork and Joyce Peterson of PPIC provided extensive editorial suggestions that improved the clarity of this report. Patricia Bedrosian of RAND also provided valuable editorial assistance.

We thank Steve Rivkin for supplying us with an algorithm to identify the California schools in our dataset. We acknowledge Aurora D'Amico, Jeffrey Owings, and Robert Atanda from the National Center for Education Statistics for supplying us with supplementary data information. We also acknowledge the many staff members at PPIC who made helpful comments along the way and who helped with the production of this report.

Finally, we are grateful to David Lyon and Michael Teitz for opening PPIC's doors to us (Julian Betts originally as a visiting fellow and Heather Rose originally as a dissertation fellow) and providing us with the opportunity to write this report.

Although our research benefited from the contributions of many people, the authors are solely responsible for any errors of fact or interpretation.

1. Introduction

A recurrent concern in the debate over education reform is that schools are not doing a good job preparing students, especially minority and disadvantaged students, to excel in school and to be successful in the labor market. This concern has led to a variety of government responses over the years, some of which have focused on curriculum. In 1983, the National Commission on Excellence in Education recommended a more rigorous high school curriculum consisting of four years of English, three years of math, three years of science, three years of social studies, two years of foreign language, and six months of computer science. Since that time, California, like other states, has taken action to enrich the curriculum offered. It has introduced content standards in a number of key subject areas over the last few years, has reintroduced state testing after a four-year hiatus, and is in the early stages of adding test components that link specifically to the content standards. Most recently, on September 30, 2000, California Governor Gray Davis approved a bill making algebra a requirement for high school graduation.

Considerable evidence suggests that differences in years of schooling explain a large portion of the income gap in the nation and in California. Naturally this leads to the assumption that the growing income gap can be narrowed by better educating people at the lower end of the income distribution, especially minority students.

But what about the courses students take: Do these matter? There is some limited evidence that students who take more math in high school are more likely to pursue postsecondary education and to have higher earnings in the future. However, it has not been established how strong these relationships are, for what groups they exist, and what else might explain the apparent effect of curriculum on postsecondary education and future earnings.

Despite the belief that an enhanced curriculum is one way to improve students' college attendance rates and earnings, the few studies that do include curriculum in estimates of these long-run student outcomes generally find minimal effects. Altonji (1995) marks one of the primary attempts by an economist to systematically establish a direct link between curriculum and wages. His work, which examined high school graduates from 1972, produced the puzzling result that the types of courses that a student takes in high school have an extremely weak effect on wages. Levine and Zimmerman (1995) find somewhat stronger results in some of their models but claim that any potential effects of math curriculum on earnings are restricted to certain subgroups of the population (low-educated men and highly educated women). The notion that the actual courses that students take in high school do not matter raises serious questions about the effectiveness of the American public school system's curriculum. Therefore, it is essential to investigate further.

Objective of the Analysis

The objective of our analysis was to answer a series of broad questions:

1. What kind of math courses do which students take? Is there a link between the type of math courses that students take, the probability that the students earn a college degree, and their future earnings?
2. If there is a link, does it reflect the effect that math courses have on students' productivity and therefore earnings, or does it merely reflect other underlying factors, such as a student's ability and motivation? (These other factors may determine both the level of math courses that a student takes and his or her future earnings.)
3. What are the policy implications of the study's findings?

For two reasons, this report focuses on the effects of the number and type of math courses that a student takes. First, research has consistently shown that math test scores are more important predictors of students' future earnings than test scores from other domains. Further, recent research by Murnane, Willett, and Levy (1995) and by Grogger and Eide

(1995) shows that between the 1970s and the 1980s, the relative importance of math test scores in determining earnings grew substantially. Despite the importance of math courses, we do broaden our analysis to include the type of courses that a student takes in other fields such as English, science, and foreign language. Our study differs dramatically from all the previous studies in that we use a very detailed dataset that allows us to measure the specific type of math courses taken, rather than just the total number of math courses.

We have chosen to focus on the relationship between math courses and earnings because a student's earnings are arguably the ultimate measure of how well schools prepare students for the labor market.

To answer the questions set forth in this report, we use the longitudinal data collected in the High School and Beyond (HSB) survey of a representative national sample of students who were in grade 10 in 1980. This survey includes detailed data from the students' high school transcripts, information about the highest educational degree the student attained, and information about earnings nearly 10 years after students should have graduated from high school. The rich demographic data, as well as information about the student's family and high school, permit us to account for many noncurriculum factors that may also be related to college graduation and earnings. Because the survey data do not contain enough California students to estimate separate statistical models for California, most of the analysis proceeds at the national level. Nonetheless, we have enough California data to perform some checks that indicate that the predictions from the national models apply to California.

Policy Relevance

From a policy perspective, a clear understanding of the effects of math courses is extremely important. This is especially true for California where, after considerable debate, Governor Gray Davis, the legislature, and the State Board of Education have decided to include algebra in high school graduation requirements and a new high school "exit" exam. Understanding the economic value to individual students of taking courses such as algebra would be useful in justifying or modifying such policies the decisionmaking process.[1]

There are also more general reasons why it is important to understand the effects of mathematics curriculum. First, to intervene in education effectively, we must understand whether students' destinies have been determined by the time they reach high school or whether a rigorous high school curriculum can alter students' paths. If it turns out that high school has little influence over student outcomes, then intervention is necessary at an earlier stage. On the other hand, if high school curriculum does affect educational and labor market outcomes, then policies aimed at encouraging students to take a more advanced curriculum may be a way of increasing the flow into college and increasing student earnings later in life.

Second, with the recent elimination of affirmative action programs in California and some other states, there is fear that minority access to postsecondary education has suffered. As the returns to a college education continue to rise, such limited access will have severe implications for income equality between different ethnic groups. In light of the disappearance of race-based admissions policies, encouraging minority students to take more math, and improving their academic foundations so that they can do so, may help to increase their enrollment in college.

Finally, if we can establish that a more rigorous curriculum indeed affects the probability of going on to college and having higher future earnings, there will be many implications for how school resources are allocated. Perhaps more money should be spent on improving curriculum options for students, as opposed to spending designed to reduce class sizes. In sum, a clear understanding of the effects of curriculum and of possible variations in these effects related to student and school characteristics will guide policymakers about how best to

---

[1]Certainly the economic value of a course should not be the sole criterion for its inclusion in the required curriculum. Nonetheless, preparing students to be successful in the labor market is one important function of schools. Therefore, it is important for schools to know the extent to which its mathematics curriculum is a vehicle for labor market and economic success.

equip students with the skills and education necessary to be successful once they leave school.

Organization of the Report

The next chapter provides an overview of mathematics course-taking behavior as well as some simple correlations between this behavior, educational attainment, and earnings. Because the policy prescription is quite different depending on the way in which curriculum affects earnings, Chapter 3 presents a theoretical discussion of the link between mathematics curriculum and earnings. Chapter 4 describes the first way in which math courses might affect earnings—by increasing students' likelihood of earning a college degree. This chapter also includes a description of the data. A more detailed data appendix augments this chapter. In Chapter 5, we turn to the more direct relationship between math curriculum and earnings, taking account of several ways in which curriculum may be operating. For the most part our analysis proceeds at the national level. Chapter 6 tests whether the results hold for certain subgroups of the sample. In this chapter, we search for variations in curriculum and outcomes between students in California and students in the rest of the nation. Chapter 7 reports the extent to which a varied curriculum can explain the ethnic and socioeconomic earnings gaps. In Chapter 8, we provide general conclusions and consider the policy implications of our results. The appendices contain many of the technical aspects of this report for readers interested in such details.

2. Patterns in Mathematics Course-Taking Behavior

The common claim that taking more math classes in high school leads to better college opportunities and higher future wages echoes in the ears of students nationwide. However, as we stated in the introduction, there is little academic research to support this claim.[1] In fact, Altonji's (1995) study finds that the economic value of the courses that a student takes during a year of high school is considerably less than the economic value of an additional year of school. These results perplexed him. The remainder of this report addresses the long-term effects of high school math courses to reconcile his results with the common belief that what students study should matter. This chapter helps to explain why the type of math courses a student takes might have an effect on earnings. It presents some background information about the type of math courses that students were taking during the late 1970s and early 1980s and shows how course-taking behavior is correlated with our two outcomes of interest: educational attainment and earnings.

Using course descriptions in the High School and Beyond transcript data, we have condensed all of the math courses a student might take in high school into six main categories. In increasing level of rigor these are vocational math, pre-algebra, algebra/geometry, intermediate algebra, advanced algebra, and calculus.[2] Using transcript data from the 1980

---

[1]Given the well-documented college earnings premium, it is understandable how courses that serve as prerequisites to college can be associated with higher earnings. However, the direct link between curriculum and earnings is much less understood.

[2]The vocational math category includes courses described as vocational math, general math, basic math, consumer math, and math review. Appendix A elaborates on the description of the remaining categories.

sophomore cohort, we determined the highest level of math each student attained.[3]

Figure 2.1 shows the proportion of *public* school students who completed a semester's worth of the given level of mathematics, as their highest level course, by the time they graduated from (or dropped out of) high school.[4] For example, 26 percent of students completed *only*

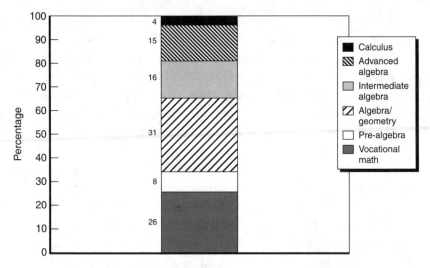

SOURCE: HSB sophomore cohort.

NOTES: Sample includes public school students who have completed at least one semester in at least one math course and are not missing any pertinent math transcript data. The highest math course is considered to be that in which the student completed at least one semester. The number of observations included is 10,073. The frequencies are weighted by the HSB transcript weight. Unweighted, the values are 26 percent, 9 percent, 30 percent, 16 percent, 16 percent, and 4 percent, respectively.

Figure 2.1—Highest Math Course Taken

---

[3]Although we refer to the *sophomore* cohort, the available transcript data include this cohort's entire high school career (from grade 9 to grade 12). We compute the highest math level as that level in which the student completed at least one semester, i.e., 0.5 standardized credits (1 standardized credit equals 1 Carnegie unit). Note, however, that in subsequent chapters on earnings models, we generally refer to a course as one lasting an entire year.

[4]This sample contains only students who completed at least one semester of a math course in high school.

vocational math courses. Another 8 percent finished pre-algebra courses, but nothing more advanced. An additional 31 percent of students stopped taking math courses after completing algebra or geometry, and only 4 percent completed the most advanced high school math course—calculus. The high percentage of students who completed only low-level courses paints a rather dismal picture of math education during the late 1970s and early 1980s. It leaves little doubt why there was such a push for curriculum reform in this period.

Long-Term Consequences

The variation in course-taking behavior had long-term implications for the welfare of these students. The number and level of math courses they completed is related to how much education they obtained overall and to how much they eventually earned. Students who completed more-advanced courses during high school tended to obtain markedly higher levels of education, and a decade after graduation they were earning significantly more than those who took only lower-level courses.

Figure 2.2 shows how the students' ultimate level of education related to their highest-level math course. In this figure, each vertical bar represents different levels of education obtained by students, with the highest level of math course indicated. For example, for the group of students who completed only a vocational-level math course, just under 15 percent did not graduate from high school, whereas nearly 50 percent graduated from high school but did not obtain any postsecondary education. Another 30 percent completed some postsecondary education, or earned a certificate or an associate's degree, but only a small number—less than 5 percent of the group—completed their bachelor's degree by 1992.

Two clear messages emerge from this figure. First, for this cohort of students, a strong positive correlation exists between the math courses that they took in high school and their ultimate educational attainment. For example, of those students who completed intermediate algebra, just over 80 percent pursued some type of education beyond high school[5]

---

[5]This includes the following educational categories: some postsecondary education (but no degree), certificate, associate's degree, and bachelor's degree.

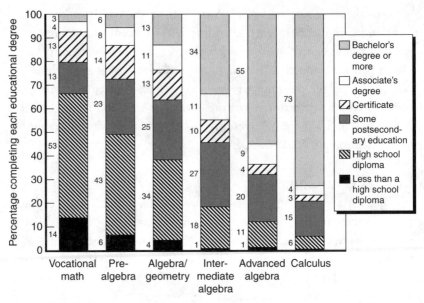

NOTES: See Figure 2.1 for the data source, sample criteria, and weighting. The sample size is only 8,850 because of missing data on educational attainment.

Figure 2.2—Highest Degree Earned by 1992 Related to Highest Math Course Taken in High School

compared to just over 30 percent of those who completed only vocational math courses.

Our second observation, which qualifies the more important result above, is that it would be a mistake to infer that postsecondary institutions shut their doors completely to those who lack "college prep" classes such as advanced algebra. Manski and Wise (1983) note that the lower tiers of four-year colleges are not particularly selective and that, in addition, the nation's large community college system allows access to postsecondary education to those who have completed high school but lack college prep classes. Figure 2.2 corroborates these claims by showing that in this cohort roughly half of those who progressed no further than pre-algebra in high school eventually obtained at least some postsecondary education.

As Figure 2.3 demonstrates, a clear upward trend in students' earnings in 1991 is associated with the level of math they experienced in high school. The median annual earnings in 1991 for students who completed calculus was $28,000 compared to $20,000 for those students who completed only a pre-algebra or algebra/geometry course and $17,000 for those who took only vocational math.[6]

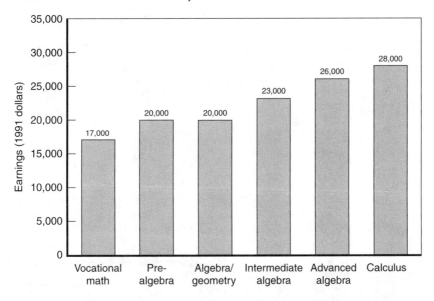

NOTES: The sample includes public school students who have completed at least one semester in at least one math course, are not missing any pertinent math transcript data, have annual earnings between $2,000 and $75,000, and are not enrolled in any postsecondary education program. The number of observations included is 5,891. The medians are weighted by the HSB fourth follow-up weights. In 1999 dollars, the above earnings are vocational math, $20,794; pre-algebra, $24,464; algebra/geometry, $28,134; advanced algebra, $31,803; and calculus, $34,250.

Figure 2.3—Median 1991 Annual Earnings, by Highest Math Course Taken

Reasons for Concern

Given the stark differences in long-term outcomes for students, the fact that a high percentage completed only vocational math is particularly

---

[6]These are 1991 dollars. Notes to the figure give the 1999 dollar equivalents.

troubling. What is even more disconcerting is that a disproportionate number of students from certain ethnic and socioeconomic backgrounds took only low-level courses, because of either their decision, their teacher's, or their school's. Such inequities contradict one of the main objectives of the American education system set forth by the *Brown v. Board of Education* decision in 1954: to offer equal opportunity to students of all races, ethnicities, and socioeconomic groups.

The dramatic variation in mathematics curriculum patterns by ethnicity is demonstrated in Figure 2.4. Almost half of the black and Hispanic students did not even take an algebra/geometry course. This is nearly double the rate for white students and almost three times the rate for Asian students.

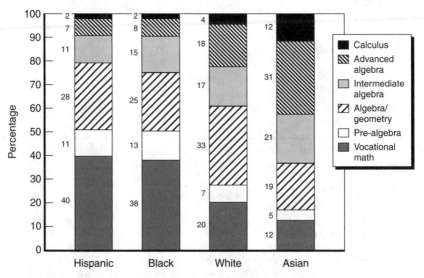

NOTES: See Figure 2.1 for the data source, sample criteria, weighting, and sample size. When these course completion rates are computed without weights, they are broadly similar to the ones above. The biggest difference is in the number of Hispanic and black students who take vocational math. In these two cases, the unweighted values are 5 percentage points lower than the weighted case, with the slack being taken up in the higher-level courses. The sample sizes for the ethnic groups are 2,221, 1,320, 5,855, and 345 for Hispanic, black, white, and Asian, respectively.

Figure 2.4—Highest Math Course Taken, by Ethnicity

Similarly, students in extremely low-income families are less likely to take advanced math courses. As Figure 2.5 shows, there was little variation in course-taking behavior among students whose parents were in the top three income brackets. However, the attrition rate is noticeably higher among students in the two lower parental income brackets, particularly in the lowest group. Whereas approximately 25 percent of students from high parental income categories did not take an algebra/geometry course, almost 60 percent of the lowest income students failed to do so.

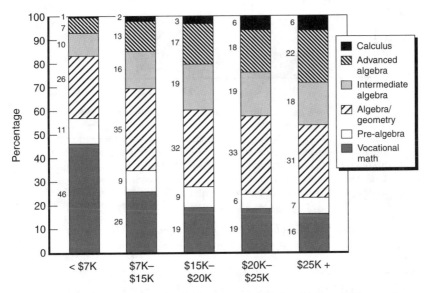

NOTES: See Figure 2.1 for the data source, sample criteria, weighting, and sample size. The sample sizes for the income groups are 916, 2,833, 1,751, 1,503, and 2,258, respectively, from the lowest to the highest income category. The income categories are in 1980 dollars. The 1999 dollar equivalents are roughly double the 1980 values.

Figure 2.5—Highest Math Course Taken, by Parental Income

The Case of California

Because California has the largest student population of any state, it is interesting to see how it compared to the rest of the nation in terms of mathematics education. As is apparent in Figure 2.6, there were no

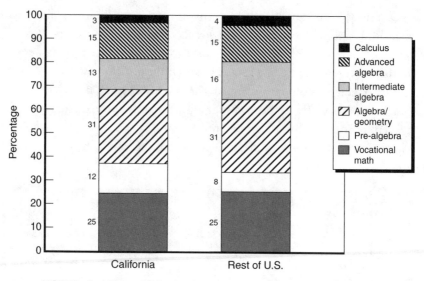

NOTES: See Figure 2.1 for the data source, sample criteria, weighting, and sample size. Additionally, those observations for which the high school's state could not be determined were omitted from the sample. There are 1,087 students from California schools in this sample and 8,303 from non-California schools. Unweighted, the U.S. percentages are 25, 8, 30, 16, 16, and 4, respectively, starting with vocational math. Unweighted, the California percentages are 22, 12, 31, 14, 18, and 4, respectively, starting with vocational math.

Figure 2.6—Highest Math Course Taken in California and the Rest of the United States

meaningful differences for students in California and students in the rest of the United States. At least for the sample of students shown (who were in grade 10 in 1980), California and the other states experienced similar trends in course-taking behavior. So although most of the analysis in subsequent chapters is concerned with results at the national level, the similarities between students in California and students in the rest of the nation help assure us that the results we find at a national level apply to California as well.

Conclusions

A substantial percentage of students stopped taking math courses at an early stage. In addition, course-taking behavior varied dramatically by ethnicity and socioeconomic status. Minorities and students from low-income families took fewer advanced courses.

This would not constitute a problem if it had no long-term consequences. However, the high school math courses that a student takes appear to be strongly related to the highest educational degree the student obtains and to earnings 10 years after high school. Although this association does not necessarily imply causality, such statistics raise a red flag, indicating the need for rigorous statistical analysis of the question. The following chapters provide the results from our more in-depth analysis.

3. How Curriculum Might Affect Educational Attainment and Earnings

Any discussion of the economic value of education generally incorporates two fundamentally different theories: human capital and signaling. The human capital theory rests primarily on the hypothesis that more schooling increases the productivity of soon-to-be workers. In contrast, signaling theory claims that schooling does not raise worker productivity but rather provides a signal to employers that a worker is more able and therefore will be more productive on the job. This chapter looks briefly at each of these theories in the context of high school curriculum and describes other mechanisms by which curriculum could affect earnings.

Human Capital Model

Human capital theory asserts that curriculum has economic value because it imparts skills to students that make them more productive and therefore better rewarded in the labor market. This mechanism can work in several ways. Take, for example, the case of mathematics curriculum (although similar arguments can be made for many subjects). Students who take more advanced math classes will learn skills that may be *directly* applicable to certain jobs. They may also learn logic and reasoning skills that *indirectly* make them more productive. In addition, skills acquired through learning advanced math may also teach students *how* to learn, so that once they are on the job, they are promoted to more demanding and more highly paid positions than those who have acquired fewer "learning skills." Finally, even if a job requires only basic math skills, a student who has taken advanced math will have had an additional chance to master those skills. For example, someone who has taken calculus has a much better grasp of algebra than does somebody who has only taken algebra, and students who have taken algebra have a much better grasp of basic skills than do students who have only taken basic math. The adage "practice makes perfect" has some merit.[1] The important thing to notice is that all of these channels for increasing wages rely on the acquisition of skills, be they direct math ability, indirect reasoning, or general learning skills that make students more productive.

Signaling Model

The signaling model offers an alternative theory as to why a more advanced curriculum leads to higher wages.[2] Consider the simple case where employers want to pay higher wages to more productive workers but cannot accurately measure productivity before hiring a worker at a given wage. If the more productive workers are those who obtain more education, then to hire more productive workers, employers simply need to observe whether their prospective employee has obtained a given level of education. In contrast to the human capital model, the signaling model assumes that math courses do not *cause* the student to be more productive. Rather, the innately more productive (i.e., "more able") students choose to obtain the specific levels of education that provide signals to prospective employers. The driving force behind this theory is that the more able students will acquire this signal because they can do so at a lower cost than the less able students. In other words, the psychic, monetary, and time costs of obtaining the signal are low enough for the more able students to incur them and still come out ahead with higher wages. However, for low-ability students, the costs are so high that they outweigh the gain in wages from providing the signal.

In the case of curriculum, the signaling model is applicable at several levels. Students who engage in a more rigorous curriculum provide a signal to colleges that they are more able. This effect is multiplied, because those who attend college will then be providing a signal to

---

[1]Gamoran (1998) mentions this phenomenon and cites other corroborating studies as well.

[2]The general signaling model was first presented by Spence (1973). See Ehrenberg and Smith (1997) for further discussion of the human capital and signaling models.

employers that they are more able than those students with merely a high school diploma. Curriculum is important in that it opens the door to college, and then college provides a signal of ability to employers. It is important to keep in mind that, according to signaling theory, none of these educational steps add to the productivity of the worker.

But what about students who do not attend college? It is less clear how taking more high school courses could act as a signal for them. The theory would assert that those who take a more advanced curriculum would signal to employers of high school graduates that they are more able than their less academically advanced counterparts. However, this presupposes that employers of high school graduates actually look at high school transcripts—an assumption not generally supported by the research of Bishop (1989). Even if employers do not actively review student records, it is conceivable that very able students (i.e., students who have taken the advanced curriculum) foresee the need to set themselves apart from their less able counterparts and thus provide information about their curriculum to prospective employers. This could take the form of additional comments on a standard application or perhaps a verbal explanation during an interview. Employers may be impressed by students who anticipate the need to provide such information and might therefore hire these more academically advanced students. However, the question still remains: Were the students hired because they are innately more able or because employers see them as potentially more productive as the result of taking more rigorous courses? If initial wages vary by curriculum, it is likely that signaling plays a role. However, if wage increases and promotions vary by curriculum, it may be more likely that actual productivity plays a role. Even in this latter case, there is still the issue that ability may be positively correlated with both curriculum and productivity and that it is ability that leads to the raise or promotion and not curriculum.[3]

---

[3]It is possible that employers do not use educational background as a signal of ability but that the student possesses some characteristic (unobservable to the researcher) that causes him or her to take a more advanced curriculum and to earn higher wages. Such a pattern would lead to endogeneity bias. This is closely related to the signaling model, because it recognizes the possibility that differences in returns from different

For policy analysts, the signaling/human capital debate is of pivotal importance. In our context, if a student gains no productivity skills by taking a specific math course but merely "buys" a signal of ability that can be sent to potential employers, then requiring all students to take that course would not raise labor market productivity. Furthermore, if less able students were forced to take that specific math course, employers would come to realize that high school students with that math course under their belts were not necessarily more able workers. The wage gain related to that math course would shrink accordingly. Furthermore, such a policy change could in fact lead to inefficiencies in the labor market because employers would now have more difficulty identifying the most productive students, because all students would now have taken the same math curriculum. On the other hand, if human capital theory is correct, then workers do become more productive after taking additional math courses. In this case, average labor productivity and wages will rise if students begin to enrich their curriculum.

Given the stark difference between the policy prescriptions produced by signaling and human capital theory, our statistical analysis of the determinants of college graduation and earnings will involve substantial robustness checks. In particular, these tests will help to break down the effect that curriculum has on earnings, so evident in the raw data, into two portions: the part due to actual increases in productivity and the part that reflects unmeasured variations in ability or motivation among students with varying degrees of math preparation.

Other Explanations of Curriculum Effects

Although the previous two hypotheses encompass many explanations of how curriculum affects wages, other mechanisms exist that are difficult to classify as one or the other. Another possible explanation is that taking more-advanced math classes causes students to channel themselves into jobs or majors that are more financially rewarding than those who do not. Although some might argue that this is a "majors" effect (or to the extent that certain majors channel students into certain occupations,

---

courses could be caused by selection effects that are the result of underlying ability. We thank Deborah Reed and Kim Rueben for this insight.

an "occupations" effect), it is important to note that such effects evolve from curriculum and should thus be attributed to curriculum. In Chapter 5, we report how much of the math curriculum effect could operate through these channels.

Similarly, advanced college math courses are prerequisites to many high-paying jobs. Students who build a strong mathematics foundation in high school may be more likely to continue their mathematics work in college and will be more successful in that work. Other students, who may be equally able, may have been discouraged from math at an early age as the result of a bad teacher, a bad experience, or trouble at home during the crucial time in which a math foundation is being laid. These able students may be bumped off the mathematics path when they are young and therefore may not even realize what future options they are forgoing. Although our analysis does not explicitly test whether students had a bad school experience, by attempting to take account of ability we show that math courses still have an effect on earnings. Therefore, one goal of a comprehensive high school should be to keep those doors open for students, so that at age 21 they are not bound by decisions made at age 11.[4]

Previous Research

A vast amount of literature has been devoted to distinguishing the human capital from the signaling effects of schooling, yet the debate is far from resolved. In Chapter 5, we address these many issues in hopes of measuring pure curriculum effects on earnings. Curriculum is rarely accounted for when modeling long-term student outcomes, such as college graduation and earnings. But one leading study (Altonji, 1995) finds that curriculum may act more as a signaling device than a form of human capital formation. Altonji concludes that "the effect of a year equivalent of courses is much smaller than the value of one year in high school." In other words, the whole is greater than the sum of its parts.

---

[4]U.S. community colleges, with their policies of open access, do provide something of a second chance for students who leave high school without the prerequisite courses for admission to a four-year college. Nonetheless, it would be more efficient for students to learn the necessary material the first time around.

For example, an additional year of math, science, and foreign language is predicted to increase earnings by 3.3 percent.[5] Because an additional year of school is estimated to increase wages by 7 percent, Altonji's results lend support to the view that high school serves as a signaling device rather than as a mechanism for human capital formation.

Our goal in this report is to understand the long-term effects of high school curriculum. Implicit in this goal is the need to disentangle the human capital effects from the signaling effects. Chapter 5 devotes the most attention to understanding the differences between these two effects. A key factor that distinguishes the present work from two earlier contributions to the literature is a detailed analysis of the *types* of math courses that students take.[6] Our subsequent analysis shows that distinguishing between types of math courses is crucial.

---

[5]These are his estimates obtained from instrumental variables. Ordinary least squares (OLS) estimates are slightly larger and OLS with high school fixed effects are substantially larger. When Altonji examines the isolated effect of mathematics, he finds that an additional year of math leads to an earnings increase of 1.8 percent, but that disappears once he controls for ability.

[6]A more thorough comparison of our research to the previous research is in Appendix C.

4. The Link Between High School Curriculum and College Graduation

As suggested in the preceding chapter, high school curriculum could affect students' long-term earnings in two ways: first, by enabling high school students to attend and graduate from college and, second, by directly increasing students' productivity in the labor market. We begin our formal analysis by examining this first question. Specifically, in this chapter we describe how taking more advanced math courses increases the predicted probability of earning a bachelor's degree. We first describe the data used for this empirical analysis and then turn to the results.

Data Description

The principal source of data for this report is the High School and Beyond (HSB) Sophomore Cohort: 1980–92 data. This longitudinal study surveys over 30,000 high school sophomores in 1980 and then follows up on approximately 15,000 of them in 1982, 1984, 1986, and 1992.[1] This is an excellent source of data for several reasons. It provides extremely detailed high school transcript information for those students in the follow-ups. These data include every course taken by the student, the term it was taken, the grade received, and the number of credits earned.[2] In addition, HSB provides earnings information sufficiently

---

[1]The first follow-up in 1982 actually includes all 30,000 students who had been selected in 1980. However, the subsequent follow-ups included only about half of the original sample.

[2]This credit measure is standardized so that a typical one-year course will be assigned 1 credit, a half-year course will be assigned 0.5 credits, a trimester course receives 0.33 credits, and a quarter course receives 0.25 credits. These standardized credits are also known as Carnegie units (i.e., 1 credit equals 1 Carnegie unit).

long after high school graduation that even those students with a substantial amount of postsecondary education can be included in the analysis. These later labor market experiences are more meaningful than the earlier ones, because students will have settled into jobs that are more representative of their likely long-term labor market path. Furthermore, a wealth of personal and family characteristics is also provided. One last important feature of these data is that even high school dropouts are included in the transcript and follow-up surveys.[3]

We constructed data on mathematics curriculum from the high school transcript data, classifying all of the math courses that the students took into one of six categories.[4] The data section of Appendix A details the system of course categorization that we use. For ease of interpretation in this chapter, we use as our curriculum measure a series of dummy variables indicating the highest level of math course taken.[5] (In the ensuing wage analysis, we use both these measures and the number of credits earned by each student in each of the six math course categories.)

In addition to detailed high school transcript data, HSB is also a rich source of postsecondary education transcript data. We do not use these data directly, as we did with the high school transcript data, but we do use the pre-calculated measure of the student's highest educational degree. We use this variable to calculate our outcome of interest in this chapter: a binary variable indicating whether the student has graduated from college.

Students for whom curriculum data are missing are excluded from our analysis. In this chapter, we exclude students for whom college graduation data are missing. Similarly, in the ensuing chapter on wages, we exclude students for whom earnings data are missing. In both cases, we include only students who attend public schools. For additional

---

[3]Respondents who miss a year are still included in the subsequent follow-up if possible. Even students who are selected into the base-year survey but miss it are included in the follow-ups if possible.

[4]Other academic subject areas were also used, but we describe math here for the sake of simplicity.

[5]We consider the highest course to be that in which the student earned at least 0.5 credits (typically a one-semester course.)

information about the data and the variables used in our analyses, see the data section in Appendix A.

Method of Analysis

We estimate the probability of graduating from college as a function of the highest math course taken by the student while in high school. The math course levels in increasing order are vocational math, pre-algebra, algebra or geometry, intermediate algebra, advanced algebra, and calculus. Of course, the observed positive relation between the highest math course and college graduation rates that we saw in Chapter 2 does not necessarily imply that there is a causal link. One possible explanation is that students with higher socioeconomic status, or who attend schools with more resources, have a head start that enables them not only to take more math in high school but also to graduate from college. To take account of such possible relationships, we control statistically for a variety of demographic, family, and school variables. We also account for the student's high school math grade point average (GPA) because of its enormous importance in the college admissions process.[6] Finally, because test scores are also an integral part of college admissions, we control for the test score that the student received on a math test administered during the sophomore year in high school. The math GPA and test score also serve as controls for the high school student's aptitude and motivation. The list of variables that we include in our model of the probability of graduating is presented in Table 4.1.

Because we are interested in only two possible outcomes—whether the student earns a bachelor's degree or not—we estimate the probability of graduating using a nonlinear probit model. The model's construction is such that it confines the predicted probabilities to a range between 0 and 1. Appendix B provides an in-depth description of the probit model and detailed results from it.

The estimated math effects in this model are striking. All of the math curriculum measures have significant positive effects on the

---

[6] GPA is often used by admissions committees to predict success at college.

Table 4.1

Characteristics Accounted for in Models of College Graduation

Probability that student graduated from a four-year college by 1992	=	F(math curriculum, demographic information, family characteristics, school characteristics)

where F(.) is a nonlinear function of the following variables:

Math curriculum	=	Series of dummy variables indicating highest math course taken
Demographic information	=	Ethnicity, gender, age in 1991, and marital status in 1991
Family characteristics	=	Parental income, parental education, parental nativity, and the number of siblings
School characteristics	=	Student-teacher ratio, books per pupil, length of the school year, size of the high school, percentage of disadvantaged students, percentage of teachers with a master's degree, district's average spending per pupil, teacher salary, whether teachers are unionized, and the school type, region, and urbanity
Student ability and motivation	=	Math GPA and grade 10 math test score

predicted probability of graduating.[7] The effects increase in magnitude as the rigor of the math course increases. In other words, the higher level the math course a student completes, the more likely he or she is to graduate from college. The same trend holds in models that are estimated separately by gender.

Because of the statistical nature of the nonlinear probit model, the magnitude of the predicted math effects varies depending on the characteristics of the student. Therefore, we present estimates of the effect of math curriculum on the predicted probability of graduating

---

[7]To ensure that taking a more advanced math curriculum leads to a higher likelihood of graduating once students arrive at college and does not represent only a higher likelihood of attending college, we estimate the original model on a restricted sample of those students who obtain some positive amount of postsecondary education. Even for this subsample of college-bound students, a more advanced math curriculum is predicted to increase the predicted probability of graduating.

from college for various groups of students. We present the math effects for an *average* student—i.e., a student for whom the values of the other conditioning variables in the model, such as socioeconomic status and school resources, are the average value of those variables for all students.

Because we are interested in how the predicted effects of curriculum vary by ethnicity and socioeconomic group, we divide our sample into 16 subgroups based on four ethnic groups (white, black, Hispanic, and Asian) and four parental-income groups (poor, low, medium, and high).[8] For each subgroup, we calculate the mean values of all of the family, school, and demographic explanatory factors of that group and use this value to typify an average student in that group. Once we have this information, we can compute the predicted probability that the average student within a specific group graduates from college, given any specific math class level. This yields a range of probabilities describing the likelihood of graduating from college given the six different levels of math courses. Figure 4.1 presents the results of our calculations.[9]

Findings

We display the results by parental income categories within the same ethnicity.[10] The points on the graphs represent the predicted probability that the average students within the specific ethnicity-income category graduate from college, given that the highest math course they completed is the value on the horizontal axis. The increase in height from one point to the next along the same line indicates the increase in the predicted probability of graduation resulting from taking the next-highest-level math course. For example, the average medium-income white student who has completed intermediate algebra has a 35 percent chance of

---

[8]We use fewer income categories here than we did in Chapter 2 for easier display. *Poor* refers to families earning less than $7,000 annually. *Low* refers to families earning between $7,000 and $20,000. *Medium* refers to those earning between $20,000 and $25,000. And *high* refers to family income categories above $25,000. (These are in 1980 dollar values.)

[9]We have included the actual table of probabilities in Appendix Table B.2.

[10]Similar analyses comparing how the probabilities vary across ethnicities within the same income group can also be made using Appendix Table B.2.

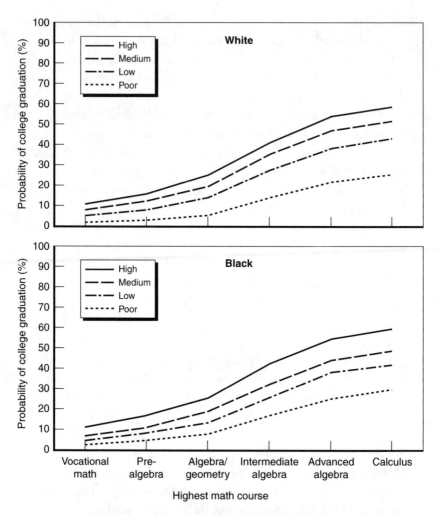

NOTES: The vertical axis denotes the predicted probability of college graduation for the average student, given the student's highest math course from the horizontal axis. The model from which these probabilities are derived controls for the demographic, family, and school characteristics listed in Table 4.1, as well as math GPA and math test score. The following income category values are given in 1980 dollars, with 1999

Figure 4.1—Predicted Probability of College Graduation Given the Stated Math Course, by Ethnicity

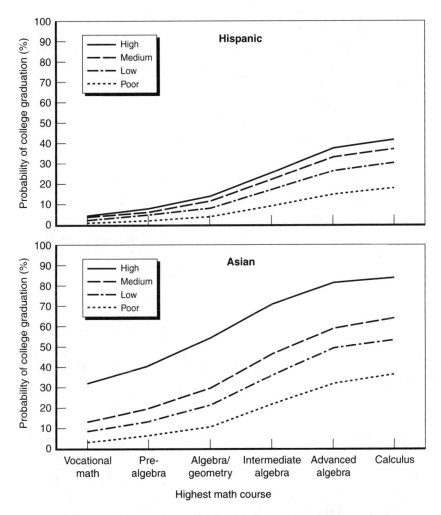

Figure 4.1—continued

graduating from college. This chance increases to 52 percent if the student has completed calculus as well.

Many interesting results hold across all ethnicities. For the average student within each of the 16 subgroups, taking more-advanced math courses is predicted to increase the probability of graduating from college. The predicted probability of graduating from college for each given level of math course is higher for the students with higher-income parents, which is hardly surprising given that relatively more disadvantaged students must overcome many more financial obstacles to attend college. For white, black, and Hispanic students, the figures suggest that curriculum matters "more" than family income in the following sense: Moving a student from the bottom to the top level of high school math course increases the student's predicted chances of college graduation more than if the student moves from the bottom to the top rung of family income.[11] Nonetheless, even though an enriched math curriculum may improve the chances of college success, it is clearly not the only ingredient.

Despite the similar results across ethnicities, there are some differences as well. For each level of math course and parental income level, Hispanics have the lowest predicted probability of graduating and Asians have the highest.

We also show similar results using an alternative measure of socioeconomic status. We categorized the students into eight categories based on the same four ethnicities and whether the students' father had earned a bachelor's degree or more. These results are presented in Figure 4.2. One of the most interesting results here is that among students whose fathers hold at least a bachelor's degree the predicted probability of graduating from college is higher for black children than it is for whites or Hispanics. It seems as if black educated parents are more successful in promoting a pro-education environment than are their white and Hispanic counterparts.

---

[11]For Asian students, curriculum is "more" effective than moving a student from the bottom to the second-highest family income category. It is worth noting that the Asian subsample is small, so the estimates are less precise than for the other ethnic groups.

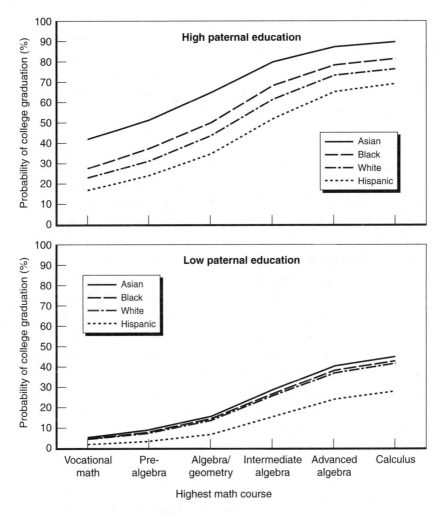

NOTES: The vertical axis denotes the predicted probability of college graduation for the average student, given the student's highest math course from the horizontal axis. The model from which these probabilities are derived controls for the demographic, family, and school characteristics listed in Table 4.1, as well as math GPA and math test score. High paternal education applies to fathers who have a bachelor's degree or higher, low paternal education refers to fathers with less that a bachelor's degree.

Figure 4.2—Predicted Probability of College Graduation Given the Stated Math Course, by Paternal Education

Conclusions

This chapter confirms an important positive relation between students' high school math curriculum and their probability of graduating from college. The results appear to apply to both men and women and to students of different ethnicities. We consider the issue that although the two are related, it is impossible to be certain that the math courses actually *cause* an increase in the probability of graduation. In other words, do math courses actually increase the likelihood of graduation, or do the students who take more advanced math courses have higher motivation or ability that would cause them to earn a bachelor's degree regardless of the type of math courses they took in high school? To provide reassurance that our results are not due to the latter explanation, we controlled for a host of potentially confounding factors, including demographic, family, and school characteristics, and also math GPA and math test score in grade 10. Because the strong links between math curriculum and the probability of graduating from college persist even after accounting for these potentially confounding factors, we conclude that there does appear to be a math effect that is not simply picking up variations in ability, motivation, or family background. In sum, it appears that math courses play an important role in predicting postsecondary education success. In the following chapter, we elaborate on this link and show how it fits into the overall picture of how math courses are related to students' future earnings.

5. The Links Between High School Curriculum and Earnings

This chapter discusses the key issues involved in estimating the effects of curriculum on earnings and presents the results of our analysis. We estimate the total effect of curriculum and then divide this effect into two parts: the indirect effect that works through the influence of curriculum on students' overall college attainment and the direct effect on earnings that is independent of whether the student graduates from college. The technical aspects of this analysis are given in Appendix C.

Key Issues in Estimating the Effects of Curriculum on Earnings

In Chapter 2, we showed that students' earnings 10 years after their expected graduation date vary systematically with their math course-taking patterns.[1] On average, students who completed more-advanced math courses had higher earnings. We also cautioned that such a trend did not necessarily imply a causal relationship between curriculum and earnings, but that it may result because of some underlying student characteristics that affect both the type of math courses a student takes and his or her subsequent earnings.

For example, we showed that the point at which students stop taking math courses varies by parental income level, with students of low-income parents dropping out of math course-taking much earlier. The low level of family resources, rather than curriculum per se, may prevent

---

[1]Because we use a cohort of the 1980 sophomore class, they are expected to graduate at the end of their senior year in 1982. We use the term "expected" to allow for the possibility that some sample members graduate early or do not graduate at all.

students from attending college and earning higher wages in the future. And, suppose that students with more highly educated parents receive strong encouragement to take a "college prep" curriculum, but that a richer curriculum itself does not "cause" wages to be higher. Instead, suppose that highly educated parents provide their children with a network of contacts and advantages outside school that leads to greater opportunities to attend an elite university, find a good first job, and so on. To separate the direct effect of curriculum from the indirect effects of parental income and education on a student's earnings, we must control for parental income and education.

Similarly, students at some schools may take a richer curriculum and later in life earn more, but better school resources, such as smaller classes and more highly educated teachers, could explain both the richer curriculum and the higher earnings of graduates. To account for this, we control for school resources.

We expect that the student's ultimate level of education has a substantial effect on earnings. As we demonstrated in the previous chapter, educational attainment is a function of high school math curriculum. To determine the effect of mathematics courses on earnings that is net of this educational attainment effect, we also control for educational attainment.

Our constant concern is that even after controlling for extensive background characteristics, any earnings effect that we attribute to curriculum may in fact result from some unobservable student characteristic (such as innate ability or motivation) that would lead to the same earnings independent of the curriculum path followed. Because of the seriousness of these issues, we devote a section of this chapter to discussing this identification problem and to presenting our attempts to control for such unobserved characteristics as ability and motivation.

Figure 5.1 shows a schematic view of these potentially confounding factors. The figure shows several characteristics that are related both to earnings and curriculum. We aim to eliminate all but one of these effects, leaving just the direct cognitive/productivity effect of curriculum on earnings.

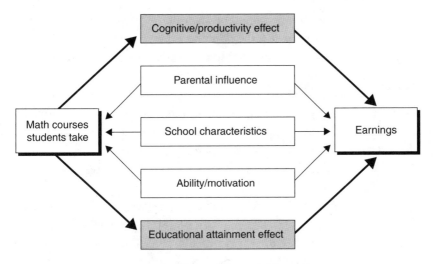

Figure 5.1—The Pathways Through Which Curriculum Affects Earnings
(and potentially confounding factors)

The Need for a Sequence of Models

With the notion of confounding factors in mind, we construct a model of earnings that accounts for a wide range of explanatory factors to minimize the chance of confounding the effects of curriculum with the effects of these other factors. Appendix C details the statistical regression analysis that we use to do this. The intuition behind this statistical approach is that we look at the difference in earnings for students who are identical except for the math courses they take. Then we attribute any difference in their earnings to the difference in their math curriculum.

To answer the question of how much math curriculum affects earnings, we need to simultaneously control for all of the factors that we discussed in the previous section. In addition to presenting the overall math effect that is net of all the other factors, we present the math effects from several intermediate models as well. We begin with a very simple model that does not take account of any student characteristics other than math courses. We then build on that model by progressively taking account of, or controlling for, the other personal and school attributes that might be responsible for the observed relation between math curriculum and earnings.

The motivation for displaying a sequence of models is that they help to show the pathway of causation. The simplest model with no controls simply restates the difference in mean earnings between workers with different numbers of math courses that we discussed in Chapter 2. Then, by controlling for family and school characteristics, we observe how much of the original math effect is due to these two groups of explanatory factors and how much is due to the characteristics for which we have not yet accounted. We will then be able to answer many interesting questions. Are the effects solely restricted to those who go on to attend college, or does math curriculum benefit those who do not attend college as well? Similarly, among college graduates, does a richer math curriculum increase wages by giving students access to college majors that are especially well rewarded in the labor market, such as engineering? To test these ideas, we account for postsecondary experience in our models and examine whether the math curriculum effects can be wholly or partially explained by college experience. Needless to say, the predicted effects of taking high school math vary across this increasingly complex set of models, but the final conclusion appears robust: Math matters.

Data

Although Appendix A presents detailed data information, we note several salient facts about our measure of earnings to supplement the data description in the preceding chapter.

The earnings data that we use are self-reported earnings from 1991. Because these earnings are measured nearly 10 years after high school graduation, even those students who obtained substantial postsecondary education will have earnings data that reflect their long-run earnings profile better than data from earlier years would have.[2] The earnings data do not explicitly measure an hourly wage (which is a much better measure of actual productivity) but rather just the aggregate earnings during the year.[3] Thus, no distinction is made between earnings from part-time and full-time work. One thing that we do to get a better idea of the productivity effect (i.e., to eliminate the hours-worked effect) is to restrict the range of incomes that we model. We eliminate those earning below a certain threshold to exclude those most likely working part-time. We restrict the range of valid annual earnings to between $2,000 and $75,000.[4] The reader should bear in mind that even with this restriction, any apparent curriculum effect may operate through two channels: an effect on wages and an effect on employment status and hours worked. It is impossible to disentangle these two effects entirely. Later in this chapter we describe another way that we try to disentangle these two effects.

We use a slightly different measure of math curriculum in this chapter than we used in the previous chapter. Rather than looking at the effect of the highest math course that a student takes, we look at the effect of the credits earned in each of six math course categories.[5] Just as we did in Chapter 2, we label the categories as vocational math, pre-algebra, algebra/geometry, intermediate algebra, advanced algebra, and calculus; a more detailed description of course content can be found in

---

[2]We exclude from our analysis students who are enrolled in some form of postsecondary education during 1991, because their earnings during that year will not necessarily reflect their long-term earnings profile.

[3]The survey did gather extremely detailed wage data until 1986 but stopped after that.

[4]In his analysis of the determinants of school quality using HSB data, Grogger (1996) restricts monthly earnings to between $500 and $6,000 (which translates into annual earnings of $6,000 to $72,000). Grogger and Eide (1995) restrict wage values to between $1 and $100 per hour (for a worker who works 40 hours a week for 50 weeks of the year; that restriction translates into annual earnings of $2,000 to $200,000). Appendix A documents the number of observations lost as a result of these restrictions.

[5]Quarter, trimester, semester, and year-long courses count as 0.25, 0.33, 0.5, and 1.0 credits, respectively. See Appendix A for more details about how we computed the number of credits from the HSB data.

Appendix A. Although our main focus is on mathematics curriculum, later in the chapter we incorporate the number of credits earned in other academic subjects such as English, science, and foreign language.[6]

Appendix Table C.1 provides summary statistics for the primary variables used in the following analysis. Table 5.1 lists the specific variables that we use in our sequence of models.

Table 5.1

Characteristics Accounted for in Models of Earnings

1991 annual earnings =	F(math curriculum, demographic information, family characteristics, school characteristics, and highest educational degree earned)

where F(.) is a linear function of the following variables:

Math curriculum	=	Math credits earned in each of six math categories
Demographic information	=	Ethnicity, gender, age in 1991, and marital status in 1991
Family characteristics	=	Parental income, parental education, parental nativity, and the number of siblings
School characteristics	=	Student-teacher ratio, books per pupil, length of the school year, size of the high school, percentage of disadvantaged students, percentage of teachers with a master's degree, district's average spending per pupil, teacher salary, whether teachers are unionized, and the school type, region, and urbanity
Highest degree earned	=	High school dropout, high school diploma, some postsecondary education (but no degree), a certificate, an associate's degree, and a bachelor's degree or higher

---

[6]As discussed above, our primary motivation for focusing on math curriculum is the strong wage-math link found by Murnane et al. (1995). Another practical reason is that the content of math courses is much more comparable across schools than is the content of courses in other subjects (see Porter et al., 1993). In other words, calculus is calculus whether one lives in the North, South, East, or West. This enables us to separate courses by their level of difficulty. Such a task is not so straightforward in other subjects that are not as uniform in content.

Results: The Effects of Math

We present the results from our sequence of models in Table 5.2, where each column represents a different model and each model contains different control variables. We report the percentage change in earnings resulting from a one-credit increase in each of the six math categories.

Table 5.2

Predicted Percentage Change in 1991 Earnings Resulting from an Additional Math Credit

	(1)	(2)	(3)	(4)	(5)
Vocational math	0.1	−1.1	−2.4**	−2.6**	−2.9**
Pre-algebra	6.9**	4.3**	2.3*	0.7	0.6
Algebra/geometry	8.4**	6.3**	6.3**	3.2**	2.7**
Intermediate algebra	11.6**	8.9**	8.2**	3.2**	2.2
Advanced algebra	14.3**	10.6**	9.2**	4.3**	3.4**
Calculus	21.5**	16.3**	12.8**	6.7**	5.8*
Control variables					
Demographic		Yes	Yes	Yes	Yes
Family		Yes	Yes	Yes	Yes
School			Yes	Yes	Yes
Highest degree earned				Yes	Yes
College major					Yes

NOTES: See Table 5.1 for a list of the demographic, family, and school control variables that we use. These percentages are not exactly equal to the regression coefficients, because the coefficients represent a first-order approximation to the proportional increase in earnings from a one-unit increase in a regressor. The exact percentage change is given by $(e^{\beta} - 1) * 100\%$, where β is the regression coefficient. Sample sizes are given in Appendix Table C.3. In this table and others throughout the report, we do not actually observe an "increase" in earnings or a "change" in earnings, because we do not observe what the earnings for a student would be had he or she not taken a particular course. Rather, we observe a "difference" in earnings between students who took a particular math course and otherwise similar students who did not. From this difference in earnings, we predict what would happen if a student took an extra math course. "Yes" indicates whether the specified control variables are in the model.

**Significant at the 5 percent level; *significant at the 10 percent level.

Effects that are statistically significant at the 5 percent level are noted with a double asterisk and those at the 10 percent level with a single asterisk. The complete regression results appear in Appendix Table C.3.

Without controlling for any other factors that might affect earnings, the effects of most math courses are quite strong and vary by the level of the course (see column 1 of Table 5.2). An additional year of calculus is predicted to increase earnings by approximately 21.5 percent, whereas an additional year of algebra or geometry is predicted to increase earnings by only about 8.4 percent.[7] Vocational math courses seem to have almost no effect on earnings.

Obviously, this first model is simplistic, because it does not take account of many other observable variables that are known to affect wages. Demographic wage differences have been well documented. In addition, many family characteristics may lead certain types of individuals to follow a certain curriculum path. Thus, it is imperative to control for these so that we do not attribute their effects to curriculum. For example, students of high-income and high-education parents may be more likely to follow a rigorous curriculum program relative to students of poorer and less-educated families, but families that place high importance on education may also be instilling values in their children that may lead to high future earnings. Results from models with the aforementioned controls are presented in column 2. (See Table 5.1 for a complete list of these controls and the controls in the subsequent models. Table C.1 provides summary statistics for these variables.) After adding the demographic and family characteristics, the math curriculum effects drop by about one-quarter but remain substantial. The curriculum effects remain different across the math course levels. A credit earned in

---

[7]These percentages are not exactly equal to the regression coefficients in Appendix Table C.3, because the coefficients represent a first-order approximation to the proportional increase in earnings from a one-unit increase in a regressor. The exact percentage change is given by $(e^\beta - 1) * 100\%$, where β is the regression coefficient. We do not actually observe an "increase" in earnings or a "change" in earnings, because we do not observe what the earnings for a student would be had he or she not taken a particular course. Rather, we observe a "difference" in earnings between students who took a particular math course and otherwise similar students who did not. From this difference in earnings, we predict what would happen if a student took an extra math course.

algebra/geometry is predicted to increase earnings by 6.3 percent, but advanced algebra is associated with a 10.6 percent gain.

Accounting for school resources and other school characteristics such as teacher education level, school size, and school location causes an additional drop in the magnitude of the curriculum effects (see column 3), suggesting that a portion of the curriculum effects from the previous model should be attributed to these school characteristics that are associated with curriculum.[8] Even after purging the school effects, all the math curriculum effects—except that of pre-algebra—are still quite large and statistically significant at the 5 percent level. Vocational math now has a significant negative effect, indicating that taking additional vocational math courses leads to lower earnings. Under human capital theory, one would expect all of the curriculum effects to be non-negative, because additional schoolwork should not hurt the productivity of students. However, in the signaling model, a negative effect is feasible because taking only low-level classes may indicate that a student is not able to perform well in the workplace. It is important to understand that in our model, the negative sign does not imply that taking an extra vocational math course actually lowers earnings relative to a student who takes no math courses. Rather, it means that taking an additional vocational math course lowers earnings relative to the average student.[9]

---

[8]Obviously, the percentage of curriculum's effect that we attribute to each group of family and school characteristics is conditional on the order in which we add these two sets of additional controls.

[9]To determine the extent to which the negative sign on vocational math is being driven by the proportion of students who take only vocational math courses and nothing higher, we re-estimated model 4 but included a dummy variable indicating whether the student had taken only vocational math (and nothing higher). The coefficient on this indicator is –0.065. The magnitude of the vocational math credits coefficient becomes slightly less negative and is –0.019. This indicates that, on average, students who take only vocational math earn less than those who take vocational math and some higher math. It also indicates that even those students who take some vocational math but also take some higher math (approximately 35 percent of the students who take one vocational math course fall into this category) still earn less than the average student who does not take any vocational math. Because the average student does not take an entire credit of vocational math, students who do take one credit are taking it at the expense of a more advanced course. This suggests that there is some opportunity cost to taking vocational math.

To further illuminate the path through which these curriculum effects work, we control for the postsecondary educational attainment of the student. Human capital models, together with the results from the last chapter, suggest that adding controls for the student's highest degree earned should reduce the effects of curriculum to the extent that college is predicted by past curriculum. Put differently, we are netting out the indirect effect of curriculum that operates through the probability of graduating from college. Of course, if the sole purpose of curriculum is to serve as a signal to colleges, so that only the most able students obtain advanced degrees, then the curriculum effects should disappear once we control for the student's highest degree.

To investigate these possibilities, we control for the student's highest educational degree attained by 1992 (refer to Table 5.1 for a list of the different degree categories). With these controls, the math curriculum effects drop by about one-half (see column 4 for the new estimates). We can interpret these *drops* from either a human capital or a signaling viewpoint. The signaling interpretation is that about one-half of the overall effect of high school math reflects the way in which math courses enable more-able students to attend college and therefore signal their ability to their employers. The human capital interpretation is that math courses in high school increase a student's efficiency, thus increasing his or her chances to attend college, and in this way increasing the student's productivity further. In the human capital interpretation, column 3 continues to show the overall effects (i.e., the productivity and educational attainment effects) of curriculum, whereas the results in column 4 show the effect that works directly through productivity rather than through education. The striking curriculum effects that remain in column 4 after controlling for educational attainment suggest that there is a direct effect of math curriculum on labor market productivity, which works independently of the final degree attained. At this point in the sequence of models, we see that the effect of pre-algebra credits is no longer statistically significant, but the high-level math effects remain significant. A course in algebra is predicted to increase earnings by 3.2

percent and a calculus course appears to increase earnings by almost 7 percent.[10]

The signs and magnitudes of the educational attainment effects are also worth mentioning and are displayed in Table 5.3. All of the

Table 5.3

Predicted Percentage Change in Earnings Resulting from Educational Attainment: Effects Measured Relative to a High School Diploma

More than a bachelor's degree	41**
Bachelor's degree	29**
Associate's degree	20**
Certificate	5**
Some postsecondary education but no degree	6**
Less than high school diploma	−13**

NOTES: These effects correspond to model 4 in Table 5.2. These percentages are not exactly equal to the regression coefficients, because the coefficients represent a first-order approximation to the proportional increase in earnings from a one-unit increase in a regressor. The exact percentage change is given by $(e^\beta - 1) * 100\%$, where β is the regression coefficient. Sample sizes are given in Appendix Table C.3.

**Significant at the 5 percent level; * significant at the 10 percent level.

---

[10]What other factors account for the 7 percent change in earnings that the model predicts for calculus? Coming from a family with a higher income (greater than $25,000) rather than coming from a family with a mid-level income ($20,000 to $25,000) is predicted to have almost the same effect as taking calculus. Furthermore, the calculus effect is almost great enough to offset the predicted negative effect of coming from a family in the extremely low income category (less than $7,000) relative to coming from a family in the $20,000 to $25,000 category. In addition, the calculus effect counterbalances the predicted effect of having a mother with less than a high school diploma rather than having a mother with a high school diploma. Are there any school resources that affect earnings as much as taking a calculus course? Not even reducing the percentage of disadvantaged students at a school by 25 percentage points outweighs the effect of taking a calculus course. See Appendix Table C.3 for the effects of all variables in the model.

attainment effects are estimated relative to the "high school only" category.[11] As expected, students with less than a high school diploma have an earnings deficit of approximately 13 percent compared to their counterparts with a high school diploma.[12] Students who have earned a certificate or participated in some postsecondary education (without earning a degree) have earnings that are, on average, 5 percent higher. An associate's degree leads to a substantial 20 percent rise in earnings. Those students who have earned a bachelor's degree experience an earnings premium of 29 percent, whereas those with an even higher degree have a 41 percent premium.

As we mentioned above, another mechanism through which curriculum could exert a positive effect on earnings is by channeling students into majors, or by keeping the door open to majors (and eventually jobs) that are more highly rewarded in the labor market. To see what portion of the curriculum effects work in this manner, we estimate a model that also controls for the student's college major. The results are displayed in column 5 of Table 5.2. Not surprisingly, many of the college majors lead to significantly different earnings from the "education and letters" major.[13] As expected, the curriculum effects all fall slightly but not enough to indicate that the bulk of the curriculum effect operated though the "college major" channel. Even with these additional controls, many of the math effects are still statistically significant.[14] Algebra/geometry yields a 2.7 percent predicted increase in earnings, whereas the predicted advanced algebra effect is stronger at 3.4

---

[11]This category was omitted from the regression model.

[12]See Appendix A for a discussion of students who obtain a general educational development (GED) diploma rather than a conventional high school diploma.

[13]The effects of the college majors can be found in the regression output in Appendix Table C.3. A detailed description of the subjects within each major is in Appendix A.

[14]To the extent that college majors are a proxy for the college courses students take, the results above mean that although college courses can explain some of the earnings differences among students, they only slightly reduce the explanatory power of high school math courses.

percent. Calculus still has the largest predicted effect at 5.8 percent, but it is now only statistically significant at the 10 percent level.[15]

In sum, it appears that the effects of curriculum seem to operate much more through the channels of educational attainment than through the choice of major. Together, judging by a comparison of columns 3 and 5, educational attainment and college major can account for approximately 55 to 75 percent of the effect of curriculum on earnings, depending on the type of math course examined. Yet even after these effects are accounted for, curriculum wields an additional influence on earnings. One potential cause may be the role that a more rigorous curriculum plays in procuring admission to more prestigious universities. Another cause may be the role it plays in opening the doors to a more advanced track within each of the majors. Finally, curriculum taken in high school may have a direct effect on labor market productivity and therefore on wages. As we suggested above, this can be the result of acquiring analytic skills that are directly applicable to certain jobs, acquiring general logic and reasoning skills that indirectly increase productivity, or by acquiring the skill of learning how to learn. Regardless of the exact cause, it is vital to note the importance of curriculum in the earnings model.[16]

---

[15]We also thought that there might be important interactions between the educational attainment variables and the majors. For example, these interactions could help us differentiate between earnings effects for physicians and medical technicians. The effect of the former is identified by a (bachelor's plus * health major) term and the latter is identified by an (associate's * health major) term. However, the effects on curriculum did not change substantially when these interactions were added.

[16]To check the stability of the results, we also estimated a model with alternative measures of earnings. Rather than using 1991 annual earnings as the dependent variable, we modified it slightly by dividing by the number of months that the person was actively employed during the year. This provides a better measure of worker productivity. At each stage, the resulting math effects were very close to those from the original model using annual earnings. Because using the monthly earnings measure meant losing many more observations resulting from missing employment data, we decided to continue using the original annual earnings values. We also experimented with different measures of curriculum. Rather than use the number of credits earned in each level of math course, we used a series of variables indicating the highest math course the student completed. The implications of the model remain unchanged. For further discussion of this alternative curriculum measure, see Appendix C.

In conclusion, we have shown that the math curriculum alone yields some important information about earnings. After taking account of demographic, family, and school traits, math courses still are predicted to affect earnings. At least half of that predicted effect on earnings operates through students' subsequent level of educational attainment and choice of college major, but some of the effect on earnings appears to operate through other avenues, such as increased productivity, as well.

Omitted Ability Variables

As we mentioned at the beginning of this chapter, we are concerned that even after controlling for extensive background characteristics, the earnings effect that we attribute to math courses could result from unobservable student characteristics that would lead to the same earnings regardless of the math courses the student took. Factors that are impossible to measure and include fully in any school-earnings study are students' innate characteristics such as ability, motivation, and drive. If we do not specifically account for these factors in our earnings model, their effects will be subsumed by the curriculum variables and we will not be able to differentiate the ability effects from the productivity effects. In other words, if we omit ability and motivation from our model, curriculum's estimated productivity effects will be larger than they should be (i.e., biased upward to the extent that these innate characteristics are positively correlated with curriculum and earnings).[17]

We adopt two main strategies to isolate the true curriculum components that are not related to ability and motivation.[18] We add

---

[17]Economic theory suggests that these characteristics are positively related both to students' level of education and to their subsequent wages. However, it is possible that a negative relation could arise between ability and education if more-able students found it optimal to leave school earlier because of the high opportunity costs of schooling in the form of forgone earnings. See Griliches (1977). Appendix C contains a technical summary describing this bias.

[18]As we pointed out in Chapter 3, employers may reward students who take a certain curriculum because that curriculum serves as a signal of the student's ability. Alternatively, high-ability students may select a more-advanced curriculum but may also possess other characteristics that are rewarded in the labor market. Because these ability and motivation characteristics are unobservable in the data and because they are related to the type of courses a student takes, higher earnings could appear to be related to curriculum when in fact they are just related to these other factors.

ability and motivation controls in the form of the student's mathematics test score, mathematics GPA, and information regarding students' and parents' attitudes toward school. We also use an instrumental variables (IV) approach similar to that used by Altonji (1995) to eliminate the part of curriculum that is related to the student's own ability and motivation. The details and results from the second estimation technique, instrumental variables, are given in Appendix C.

This section focuses on the first method, in which we attempt to separate the curriculum measures from any residual ability and motivation components by estimating models that include math test score, math GPA, and several attitudinal variables as controls. Below, we briefly describe these variables and discuss whether they satisfactorily control for ability or motivation.

Ideally, we would like a scientific, neurological measure of students' *innate* characteristics—physical features that are untouched by social, cultural, or environmental factors. Because innate characteristics are not alterable by any policy, it is especially important to eliminate all of their effects that might otherwise be attributed to some policy target, which in our case is math curriculum. Obviously, such an objective measure is impossible to obtain. At the same time, we would like to control for *acquired* skills that the student gained before high school, so as not to confuse the effect on earnings of taking a math course in high school with these previously acquired skills.

To control for both innate ability and previously acquired skills, we hoped to include a pre-high school test score to control for pre-high school math ability and prior learning experiences. Unfortunately, the earliest test score data available in HSB is from a series of tests administered during the spring semester of the student's sophomore year.[19] Because this score is likely to be affected by the curriculum studied during grades 9 and 10, it does not provide an adequate measure of pre-high school math aptitude. In particular, we note that adding this score to the model may "overcontrol" for ability, because math achievement in the spring of grade 10 is likely to be a function of math courses taken in grades 9 and 10. Therefore, its use may cause the

---

[19]Appendix A gives detailed information about this test score.

estimated curriculum effects to be lower than the true effects. Despite these shortcomings, we present models that include the grade 10 test score.

The student's math grade point average also provides a potentially good measure of ability and motivation because it represents how well students understand and apply themselves, given a particular curriculum. It is a reasonable measure of ability in that, all else equal, the more able students will earn higher scores on homework and exams than will the less able. However, grades are not strictly a function of such scores. They are often based on other non-content-related factors such as participation in class, punctuality, neatness, and behavior. Such characteristics more aptly describe motivation than true innate talent. In this respect, including GPA in the model of earnings accounts for the motivation that could influence student's future earnings. Further, parental supervision of homework and study habits surely affects how well students do in their classes, regardless of the students' true ability. Such parental involvement and guidance in their children's education has a strong cultural base, which to some extent may be accounted for by the parental characteristics that we include in the model (such as income, education, and nativity). Nonetheless, GPA may be capturing some of the parental involvement effects. Although the effect of GPA may not uniquely be an ability or a motivation effect, it does allow us to account for this conglomerate of effects that may have some bearing on future earnings.

One final drawback worth mentioning about GPA is that it can be affected by math course level, and therefore the direction of its effect on earnings is not obvious. High-ability students who take the highest-level math course may wind up with a lower GPA than their counterparts who only take medium-level math courses because it may be more difficult to earn a higher grade in the most rigorous courses. In this case, if we cannot completely control for ability, lower GPAs could be associated with higher earnings. GPA may also affect earnings because, even among all college-bound students, those with higher GPAs gain admission to the more prestigious colleges that carry an earnings premium.[20]

As an additional way to account for student motivation and parental influence, we also control for a set of attitudinal variables that indicate the academic inclination of students and parents. These variables indicate whether the parents closely monitor the student's schoolwork, whether the parents know where their children are at all times, whether the student intends to go to college, the amount of television the student watches, and how much time the student spends reading outside of class. Although such measures are subjective, they offer a possibility of controlling for a student's motivation and attitudes toward schoolwork.

Considering the difficulty in distinguishing one effect from the other, for expositional purposes we refer to the ensemble of ability, motivation, and attitude as "ability." The results from adding these ability controls are presented in Table 5.4. We compare them to the original model that included controls for highest degree, but not for major.[21] We redisplay the results from this baseline model in column 1 for easier comparison. In columns 2, 3, and 4, we add the math GPA, the math test score, and the attitudinal controls separately. Column 5 shows the results from adding the math GPA and math test score simultaneously. Column 6 shows the estimates from adding all three controls at once. For each model, the table shows the percentage change in earnings associated with an increase of one credit for each of the math courses. More detailed regression results are given in Appendix Table C.4.

The results are fairly consistent regardless of the individual ability control that we use. The algebra/geometry math effects appear significant and of approximately the same magnitude in all cases. An additional course in algebra or geometry is predicted to lead to a 2.5 to

---

[20]For evidence that universities vary in quality in ways that are systematically related to the average achievement of college freshmen as well as measures of the quality of the university teaching force, see Morgan and Duncan (1979), James et al. (1989), Rumberger and Thomas (1993), and Daniel, Black, and Smith (1997).

[21]The original model is shown in column 4 of Table 5.2.

Table 5.4

Predicted Percentage Change in Earnings Resulting from an Additional Math Credit with Various Ability Controls Included

	(1)	(2)	(3)	(4)	(5)	(6)
Vocational math	−2.6**	−2.9**	−2.3**	−2.7**	−2.7**	−3.2**
Pre–algebra	0.7	0.5	0.6	0.2	0.5	−0.2
Algebra/geometry	3.2**	3.0**	2.6**	3.3**	2.6**	2.5**
Intermediate algebra	3.2**	2.2	1.8	2.4	1.2	1.2
Advanced algebra	4.3**	2.9**	2.8*	3.6**	1.9	1.3
Calculus	6.7**	4.8	5.7*	6.7**	4.6	4.6
Ability controls						
Math GPA		3.7**			3.4**	3.7**
Math test score			0.3**		0.2	0.1
Attitudes				Yes		Yes

NOTES: All models control for demographic, family, school, and educational attainment characteristics. See Table 5.1 for a complete list. These percentages are not exactly equal to the regression coefficients, because the coefficients represent a first-order approximation to the proportional increase in earnings from a one-unit increase in a regressor. The exact percentage change is given by $(e^\beta - 1) * 100\%$, where β is the regression coefficient. The model in column 1 is the same as the model in column 4 of Table 5.2. Sample sizes are given in Appendix Table C.4. "Yes" indicates whether the specified control variables are in the model.

**Significant at the 5 percent level; *significant at the 10 percent level.

3.3 percent increase in earnings—similar to the case with no ability controls. Similarly, the advanced algebra effect remains statistically significant at the 5 percent level when we add math GPA or attitude controls and at the 10 percent level when we add the math test score; however, it does drop somewhat in magnitude from the case of no ability controls. The calculus coefficient remains significant at the 5 percent level when we add attitude controls, but it is only borderline significant when we control for the math test score and is no longer significant when we add the math GPA. Adding the controls jointly does not alter the results much. The algebra/geometry and the vocational math effects remain significant, but the advanced algebra effects fall to insignificant levels.[22]

We prefer the model that controls for math GPA because we retain the regression sample almost in its entirety and the other controls do not lead to substantially different results. However, it is important to note that such results should be interpreted with caution, because the GPA coefficient may be picking up some of the curriculum effect, leading to an understatement of the effect of curriculum. Nonetheless, we think that math GPA is less prone to "overcontrolling" than the math test score.

Results: The Effects of Other High School Subjects

Although our research focuses primarily on the effects of mathematics curriculum, we do extend it to cover the effect of other subjects. Specifically, we incorporate English, science, and foreign language curriculum measures into our model because they make up the core academic courses.[23] However, one problem that arises when we add these curriculum measures is their collinearity with math. The number of math credits earned has a correlation of 0.54, 0.36, and 0.38 with science, English, and foreign language credits, respectively. This makes it more difficult to truly isolate the effect that math has on earnings independent of these other subjects. Nonetheless, we still find very pronounced math effects as well as effects from courses in these additional subjects.

We incorporate the additional subjects into the model using detailed curriculum categories as before. We classify the number of credits earned in English courses into four levels: below grade level, average grade level, above grade level, and English literature courses. The science curriculum is measured as the number of credits earned in each of six science course

---

[22]The size of the effects may be changing across model specifications in part because of the falling sample sizes that result from missing data in some of the controls. When we include the math test score, we lose 13 percent of the regression sample resulting from missing test score data.

[23]We also estimated models that included social science credits, but the main results were not altered. We decided to leave social science credits out to reduce collinearity problems.

categories.[24] We classify foreign language curriculum into two variables. One designates whether the student took one or two courses whereas the other signals that the student took three or four courses. Thus, these two effects are measured relative to the effect of taking no foreign language courses at all.[25]

The results from this new model containing all four subjects are presented in Table 5.5. We omit math GPA from these models and rely primarily on the instrumental variables estimator (the results of which are in Appendix C) to eliminate the ability/motivation portion of the curriculum effects. Furthermore, the other subjects may also serve as ability and motivation controls when we are trying to ascertain the true math effect. For instance, it may be that only the most able and ambitious students complete three or more years of foreign language study. We also exclude math GPA, because without including GPAs for the other subjects, the relative earnings effects of math to the other subjects will be distorted. All models include controls for demographic, family, and school characteristics as well as the highest educational degree attained by the student. Detailed OLS regression output as well as the IV results are given in Appendix Table C.6.[26]

To help illustrate the changes that occur by including the additional curriculum measures, in column 1 of Table 5.5 we present the predicted math effects from the model that includes only math credits in the curriculum measures.[27] Including the curriculum measures from other subjects (see column 2) causes the math effects to drop by approximately

---

[24]As with the math classification scheme, these are based on the categorization obtained from the U.S. Department of Education, the details of which can be found in Appendix A.

[25]We exclude "English as a second language" courses from the foreign language category.

[26]IV is an alternative method for controlling for ability and is described in Appendix C.

[27]This was originally presented in column 4 of Table 5.2. It is also interesting to compare the results from this new model to the results from the basic model that also controls for math GPA (i.e., the model in column 2 of Table 5.4). The high-level math effects in both of these models are quite comparable and indicate that the additional curriculum measures might be picking up an ability/motivation effect in the same way that GPA does.

Table 5.5

Predicted Percentage Change in Earnings Resulting from Specific Math, English, Science, and Foreign Language Courses

	(1)	(2)
Vocational math	−2.6**	−3.0**
Pre-algebra	0.7	0.4
Algebra/geometry	3.2**	2.0*
Intermediate algebra	3.2**	1.9
Advanced algebra	4.3**	3.0**
Calculus	6.7**	4.4
Below-grade-level English		0.4
Average English		1.5**
English literature courses		1.5*
Above-grade-level English		2.6**
Basic biology		−0.8
General biology		−1.5
Primary physics		−2.3**
Secondary physics		0.5
Chemistry 1, physics 1		2.0
Chemistry 2, physics 2, advanced placement biology		2.0
Foreign language (1–2 credits)		2.5
Foreign language (3–4 credits)		5.5**

NOTES: All models control for demographic, family, school, and educational attainment characteristics. See Table 5.1 for a complete list. These percentages are not exactly equal to the regression coefficients, because the coefficients represent a first-order approximation to the proportional increase in earnings from a one-unit increase in a regressor. The exact percentage change is given by $(e^\beta - 1) * 100\%$, where β is the regression coefficient. The model in column 1 is copied from the column 4 model of Table 5.2 for easy comparison between the original math effects before we account for ability and the math effects once we control for other subjects. Another interesting comparison is the one between the model with additional subjects and the math-only model where we control for math GPA (see column 2 of Table 5.4). The math effects are very similar in these two cases, indicating that including subjects in other courses may be a way of controlling for motivation and ability.

**Significant at the 5 percent level; *significant at the 10 percent level.

30 to 40 percent from the base level case, depending on the math course (except for the case of vocational math). It is interesting to note that the advanced-level English credits are predicted to have a larger effect on earnings than are average-level English credits. It appears that taking an advanced-level English course increases wages by more than an additional course in algebra, geometry, or intermediate algebra does, but by less than the more-advanced math courses do. Average-level English credits, on the other hand, lead to smaller increases in earnings than do any of the math courses at or above the algebra/geometry level. None of the science effects are statistically significant except for the low-level science, primary physics, which is predicted to have a negative effect on earnings (most likely for the same reasons that vocational math does). Taking three or four foreign language courses also has a significant positive effect. At 5.5 percent, its effect seems relatively large compared to those of other subjects; however, it represents the effect of *three to four* credits whereas the predicted effects of the other subjects represent the effect of *one* additional credit.

Our results indicate that the mathematics curriculum has a large effect on earnings, regardless of whether we also control for other types of courses taken. Furthermore, contrary to Altonji's findings, we find that the sum of the parts (i.e., the effect of high school courses) is approximately equal to the whole (i.e., the effect of an additional year of high school, often cited as a 7 percent increase in earnings) for a student who has completed an average-level high school curriculum. For a student who takes a more advanced curriculum, the sum of the parts, perhaps as expected, can be greater than the whole . This can be seen best by considering some simple thought experiments.

To compare our estimated effects of a year's worth of curriculum to the 7 percent effect of a year's worth of schooling, Table 5.6 shows OLS estimates of potential combinations of high school curriculum during the last two years of school. The first row shows that students who drop out in grade 10 experience a 13 percent earnings deficit compared to those who stay in school (calculated as the effect of having less than a high school diploma in Table 5.3). This resonates with the estimated 7 percent benefit per year that school provides. For students who do not drop out,

Table 5.6

Predicted Earnings Effect of Hypothetical Course Combinations During Grades 11 and 12

School Year and Level	Hypothetical Curriculum	Predicted Effect (%)
10 drop out	No more subjects	−13.2**
11 low	No math, average English, secondary physics, no foreign language	2.1
11 medium	Intermediate algebra, average English, chemistry 1, foreign language (third year)	7.0**
11 high	Advanced algebra, advanced English, chemistry 1, foreign language (third year)	9.4**
12 low	Same as grade 11 low	2.1
12 medium	advanced algebra, English literature, chemistry 2, physics 1	8.9**
12 high	Calculus, advanced English, chemistry 2, foreign language (fourth year)	10.8**

NOTES: Because we are using the log of earnings rather than actual earnings as the dependent variable in our regression analysis, the percentages in this table are only approximately equal to the sum of the individual effects of the hypothetical class list from column 2 of Table 5.5. Because we are looking at the effect of changes in more than one of the explanatory variables, the technical way that we compute these percentages is to first sum up the actual regression coefficients from the model in column 2 of Table C.6. This model controlled for demographic, family, school, and educational attainment characteristics and was estimated with OLS. Then, we convert the sum to a percentage change in earnings by taking the exponential of that sum, subtracting 1, and multiplying by 100 percent. We determine whether the effects are significant by using the coefficients and standard errors from the regression model in column 2 of Table C.6. The standard errors of the hypothetical predicted effects are computed by taking the square root of the variance of the sum of the coefficients from the hypothetical class list. To compute the effects more easily, we estimate a slightly different specification of the column 2 model in which we enter the total number of foreign language credits rather than the two dummy variables. Coefficients on the other subjects are practically unchanged. That of foreign language credits becomes 0.014.

**Significant at the 5 percent level.

we present three hypothetical course loads (low, medium, and highly academic combinations) that they could take during grade 11 and similarly for grade 12. The table demonstrates that returns to curriculum depend critically on the type of courses a student takes. A low-level curriculum has a predicted effect on earnings of about 2 percent. Students with a medium-level curriculum achieve close to a 7 percent increase in earnings for each year's worth of their curriculum. However, those with a high-level curriculum actually surpass that level and experience an earnings premium closer to 9 or 10 percent for each additional year of education.[28]

Conclusions

The work in this chapter has demonstrated that math curriculum seems to have a substantial effect on earnings well after high school graduation. Depending on the specific math course, the basic linear models show that one-half to three-quarters of the math effect operates through the channels of educational attainment and choice of college major.[29] A portion of the remaining math effect appears to be due in part to the correlation among student's ability, motivation, curriculum, and earnings. In other words, highly motivated and able students, who would earn higher wages in the future regardless of their high school curriculum, happen to follow a more rigorous math program. Both methods of accounting for this underlying relationship—ability controls and instrumental variables—yield a similar result: Math effects do diminish but are still important. Adding GPA to control for motivation causes each specific math effect to decrease slightly. The high-level math effects drop by more than the algebra/geometry effect does, resulting in

---

[28]Throughout this exercise, we assume that all other background characteristics are held constant and that the only difference between the students we are comparing is their curriculum. In other words, the effects within each academic year (e.g., grade 12) are measured relative to a hypothetical student who stays in school that academic year but does not take any math, English, science, or foreign language courses. The more interesting comparisons are between students who take a high-level curriculum rather than a low-level curriculum.

[29]We arrive at these proportions by comparing the linear model that controls for demographic, family, and school traits to one that also controls for highest degree earned and another that additionally controls for college major.

an algebra/geometry and an advanced algebra effect that are of similar magnitudes. The effect of calculus still appears to be larger than the other math effects and the effect of vocational math is still much lower.[30] For the most part, these results withstand the addition of other high school subjects to the model.

One aspect of the above analysis makes it unique among published research on curriculum and earnings: It is the first analysis that classifies the number of math courses that students take based on the academic level of the course. In doing so, we arrive at much more accurate estimates of mathematics effects than previous researchers have been able to do. We conclude that math does matter. We would not have found these results had we used the aggregate number of math courses taken by the student rather than the actual level of the math courses. We elaborate on this point in Appendix C, but note here that this finding has many implications for curriculum reform. Merely increasing the number of courses required of students may not achieve the desired effect. It will be important to focus on the type of courses students are required and motivated to take as well.[31] In particular, our results suggest that algebra/geometry courses should be a fundamental part of any curriculum reform.

---

[30]On the other hand, using instrumental variables predicts that algebra/geometry courses tend to have the biggest positive effect on earnings (nearly 6 percent) and vocational math seems have the same size effect but in the negative direction.

[31]When graduation requirements are increased, there is the potential risk of more students dropping out. (See Costrell, 1994, and Betts, 1998, for a theoretical analysis and Lillard, 1998, for an empirical analysis.)

6. Variations in Math Effects Among Subgroups of Students

Even after controlling for a wide array of factors, high school math curriculum appears to influence students' earnings about a decade after graduation. Do these results suggest that a rich math curriculum would benefit all students equally, or are the benefits limited to certain subsamples of students?

In this chapter, we first examine whether the results that we find at a national level apply to California students. Next, we discuss whether the math effects are similar for various subsamples of workers based on their gender. We then investigate whether certain student characteristics and measures of school resources influence the effectiveness of the math curriculum. Finally, we discuss whether the math effects might depend on the student's ultimate level of education.

Math Effects in California

For California policymakers, it would be useful to know whether the results we find at the national level also apply to California. California is an interesting case study for the rest of the nation as well. It has the largest population of students of any state and is in some respects a leader in education policy. If it enacts major changes in curriculum, the rest of the nation may follow.

Ideally, we would like to reproduce the statistical analysis in this report for the subsample of Californian students so that we can determine whether the relationship between mathematics course-taking behavior and earnings is the same for this state as it is for the nation. The problem with estimating a separate model for California is that the sample size of California students in the transcript data we have is too small to obtain accurate estimates (there only 630 Californian observations and just over 60 explanatory factors in our model). Because we cannot precisely estimate the math effects for California students in a separate model, we perform two procedures to determine how the national models might compare to a California model. We discuss the results below, deferring the technical details to Appendix D.

First, we re-estimate the model of math effects, adding a series of control variables that permit the math effects to vary depending on whether the student attended a California high school. We find that any additional California math effect is statistically indistinguishable from zero.

The above model constrains the effects of the non-math explanatory variables to be the same both in and out of California. However, the estimated math effect is also determined in part by the way in which math curriculum covaries with these other variables. So, we also test whether the relationship between the math curriculum variables and the remaining explanatory variables is the same in the California sample as it is in the rest of the nation. We find that it is the same.

Math Effects and Gender

One concern that comes to mind is whether the effects we found in the previous chapters are comparable for men and women. Course-taking behavior is actually quite similar between men and women, so it would be useful to see if curriculum has similar effects for both genders.[1] Because our results indicate that much of the curriculum effect operates through the channel of educational attainment, in this section we present the results from a pair of separate earnings models for each gender. The first model does not control for educational attainment, which means that the math effects contain both a direct cognitive/productivity effect and an educational attainment effect. The second model does take account of the student's ultimate level of education, leaving just the

---

[1]On average, males earn somewhat more credits in vocational math than females do (means of 0.82 and 0.56, respectively) and females earn slightly more than males in algebra/geometry courses (mean of 1.0 versus 0.9). The remaining gender-specific means are within 0.01 of the pooled means (see Table C.1 for the pooled summary statistics). Another way to think about this difference is that slightly more males than females stop taking math at the vocational math level (29 percent versus 23 percent) with most of the difference being made up at the algebra/geometry level.

direct cognitive/productivity portion of the math effect. Once again, this series of models allows us to see the path through which curriculum works. Both sets of models control for the standard demographic, family, and school characteristics that we use throughout the study, as well as the student's math GPA. Table 6.1 displays the results from this exercise. The full set of regression results is displayed in Appendix Table D.1.

The effect of curriculum is quite strong for men in models that do control for GPA but do not control for educational attainment. Column 1 of Table 6.1 shows that an additional credit earned in the algebra/geometry category is predicted to increase earnings by 3.7 percent, whereas additional intermediate and advanced algebra credits have even larger predicted effects—5.9 percent and 4.9 percent, respectively.[2] Controlling for the student's ultimate level of education diminishes these effects substantially, suggesting that a large part of the

Table 6.1

Predicted Percentage Change in 1991 Earnings Resulting from an Additional Math Credit, by Gender

	Male		Female	
	(1)	(2)	(3)	(4)
Vocational math	–2.4*	–2.6**	–3.9**	–3.9**
Pre-algebra	0.9	0.1	2.2	0.5
Algebra/geometry	3.7**	1.2	7.5**	4.6**
Intermediate algebra	5.9**	2.4	5.2**	1.4
Advanced algebra	4.9**	1.5	8.5**	5.0**
Calculus	4.2	0.9	14.4**	9.4*
Math GPA	6.2**	4.1**	5.5**	3.6**
Highest degree earned	No	Yes	No	Yes

NOTES: Standard errors are in parentheses. All models contain controls for demographic, family, and school characteristics. See Table 5.1 for a complete list. "Yes" indicates whether the specified control variables are in the model.

**Significant at the 5 percent level; *significant at the 10 percent level.

---

[2] These effects are statistically significant at the 5 percent level.

gains to taking math courses in high school for men come through higher educational attainment. None of the effects remain statistically significant except that of vocational math, which is negative.[3]

The predicted effect that math curriculum has on earnings is much larger for women than for men, regardless of whether we control for educational attainment. In the model that does not control for highest degree earned, the predicted effects are almost double those for men. An additional credit in algebra/geometry is predicted to increase women's earnings by 7.5 percent and an additional credit in advanced algebra by 8.5 percent. After controlling for the student's highest educational degree, these effects drop to 4.6 percent and 5.0 percent, respectively.[4] One explanation for why the effects may be larger for women than for men is that they may be capturing a labor force selection effect that tends to be stronger for women. Perhaps women who take more advanced high school math earn more per hour *and* work more hours, but men who take advanced math courses only earn more per hour. To the extent that the curriculum effect includes both productivity and labor force attachment, it will tend to be larger for women.

Math Effects and School and Student Characteristics

Another question that we would like to be able to answer with our research is: Do certain school and student characteristics make mathematics curriculum more or less effective? For example, do schools with high percentages of disadvantaged students bestow the same math

---

[3]Repeating this pair of models but excluding GPA from both leads to predicted math effects that are somewhat stronger. Without including highest degree, the same math effects are statistically significant but larger in magnitude. In addition, the calculus coefficient is significant at the 10 percent level. More interesting, once we control for highest degree, the intermediate and advanced algebra coefficients are significant at the 10 percent level with values of 0.035 and 0.031, respectively. One more point of note is that in the model that does not control for GPA or highest degree earned, the vocational math coefficient is no longer significantly different from zero.

[4]The calculus effect is significant at the 10.6 percent level, and when GPA is not included in the model it is significant at the 5 percent level. The other significant coefficients remain significant without GPA in the model but tend to be larger in magnitude.

benefits on their students that more affluent schools do? Do students of different ethnicity benefit from a given curriculum to varying degrees?

To some extent, we have been able to get at the answer by controlling for many of the school and student qualities that may influence curriculum's effects. Ideally, we would like to have a large enough sample of any particular population of interest (e.g., inner-city schools with characteristics x, y, and z) so that we could estimate a model using that subsample. However, with the available national datasets, this is not feasible. Appendix D describes how we attempt to test whether there are any interaction effects between math curriculum and student and school characteristics; we briefly summarize the results of these tests below.

The effect of math courses on earnings does not appear to vary with respect to student characteristics, characteristics of the student body at the high school, or measures of school resources. This conclusion reinforces the results in our previous chapter as it shows that a rigorous math curriculum at *any* school can benefit students of *any* type.

Nevertheless, there may be some possible exceptions. There is some weak evidence that math effects are strongest for disadvantaged students, those from lower-income families, and those at schools at which students on average take a less-rigorous curriculum. Why would students from more-advantageous backgrounds benefit less from math curriculum? One explanation is that they have the family and social infrastructure in place that will help them succeed regardless of their curriculum. Thus, curriculum does not really make or break these students' later careers. Curriculum really seems to make a big difference for students who may not have these other safety nets.

Math Effects and Educational Attainment

Despite the presence of strong predicted mathematics curriculum effects in the previous chapter, a natural extension to our model is to analyze whether the math effects that we observe are restricted to certain educational attainment groups. Given Bishop's finding (1989) that employers typically do not read high school transcripts, curriculum might not matter for high school dropouts or for those who obtain no postsecondary education. For college graduates, one would expect the signaling returns to curriculum to disappear after controlling for educational attainment.[5] Yet, our results show that even after controlling for the highest degree attained, math curriculum effects are still present and strong, suggesting the presence of human capital effects. Even with additional testing, described in Appendix D, we found very little evidence that the curriculum effects depend on the student's ultimate level of education.

Conclusions

Although we were unable to estimate a separate model for the subsample of California high school students, through a series of analyses we have gained confidence that the results from the national model do apply to California students as well.[6]

Math curriculum is predicted to affect earnings significantly for both men and women. However, for men, unlike women, most of the effect of curriculum appears to work through the effect of math courses taken in high school on the student's ultimate level of educational attainment.

Another important component of this chapter discussed whether student or school characteristics mediate the effectiveness of curriculum in increasing earnings. This is a crucial concern for policymakers, who will want to know whether, for instance, the math curriculum offered at affluent schools with many resources and largely upper-income white students will prove as effective in a different school and socioeconomic environment. With some possible exceptions, most student and school characteristics do not seem to alter the effect of math curriculum. Furthermore, there do not appear to be any significant differences in the effect of math curriculum for students of different educational

---

[5]If no education controls are in the model, high school curriculum may be a proxy for the college signaling effect.

[6]Because HSB surveys students for the first time in their sophomore year, it undercounts dropouts (especially Hispanic dropouts who are more likely to leave school before grade 10) and immigrants who never attend U.S. schools. Given this undercount and the small California sample, we cannot say definitively that there are no differences inside California.

attainments. It is worth keeping in mind that the evidence supporting these last two results is weak, yet we mention them as a point for further policy discussion and research.

7. Math Curriculum and the Earnings Gaps Among Ethnic and Socioeconomic Groups

As we demonstrated in Chapter 2, math course completion rates vary considerably by ethnicity. Minorities are overrepresented in low-level math courses and are underrepresented in higher-level math courses. Nearly 9 percent of Hispanic students and 10 percent of black students complete math credits at the advanced algebra level or higher,[1] but these completion rates pale in comparison to the rates of 22 percent and 43 percent for white and Asian students, respectively.[2] These patterns are also apparent if we look at the number of credits earned rather than the highest course completed. Asians and whites tend to earn fewer credits in vocational and pre-algebra math courses than do Hispanic, black, and Native American students. Conversely, these minorities earn fewer credits in all math classes at or above the algebra/geometry level.

Discrepancies in math course-taking patterns are also apparent for students of varied parental income levels. Drawing from our Chapter 2 results, students from the lowest-income families (those whose parents earn less than $7,000 annually) are concentrated in the lower-level math courses, with 46 percent failing to progress beyond vocational math. For students from middle-income families (those earning $20,000 to $25,000) only 19 percent fail to advance beyond that level. Whereas 24

---

[1]This includes students who complete credits in advanced algebra *or* calculus.

[2]We refer to the percentages from Chapter 2 in which we include every possible public school observation for which we have race and math data. The same course-taking trends documented in Chapter 2 are evident for the weighted regression sample as well.

percent of middle-income students take courses at or above the advanced algebra level, only 8 percent of the lowest-income students do.

In light of these disparities in curriculum, this chapter asks: How much of the earnings gap between members of different ethnic groups or parental income groups can be attributed to these variations in mathematics course-taking behavior? The first column of Table 7.1 reports the ethnic earnings gaps for the 1991 earnings of the HSB sophomore cohort. The percentages indicate the difference between average earnings for workers in the specified ethnic group and white workers. Hispanic and black workers earn less than whites, on average—

Table 7.1

Percentage Earnings Gap Based on Ethnicity Difference in 1991 Earnings Relative to White Workers

	(1)	(2)	(3)
Native American	−20.4**	−9.7**	−6.6
Black	−9.5**	−1.0	−0.02
Hispanic	−5.0**	1.0	3.7*
Asian	9.6**	7.4*	2.3
Other controls			
Curriculum	No	No	Yes
Demographic	No	Yes	Yes
Family	No	Yes	Yes
School	No	Yes	Yes

NOTES: The effects of ethnicity are measured relative to whites. Column 1 represents a simple model of 1991 annual earnings explained by ethnicity only. There are no other controls in this model. Columns 2 and 3 represent models that control for demographic, family, and school characteristics. The specific variables in each of these categories can be found in Table 5.1. The model in column 3 also controls for curriculum. The change in the ethnic effects from column 2 to column 3 represents the portion of the earnings gap that curriculum can explain. "Yes" indicates whether the specified control variables are in the model.

**Significant at the 5 percent level; *significant at the 10 percent level.

about 5 percent and 9.5 percent less, respectively.[3] The asterisks indicate that the gaps are statistically different from zero. We established the magnitude of the ethnic earnings gaps by estimating a model of earnings that controls only for the ethnicity of the student. Detailed regression results for this and subsequent models in this chapter are presented in Appendix Table E.1.

There are also large earnings gaps between students of different socioeconomic backgrounds. The first column of Table 7.2 documents the earnings gap for students who come from families of different income levels. The percentages represent the difference in average earnings between workers from the specified family income level and workers whose parents are from the middle-income category, i.e., families that earned between $20,000 and $25,000 a year in 1980.[4] Students in the lowest-parental-income category (less than $7,000) earned 25.4 percent less than students from middle-income families in 1991. Students in the next-lowest-parental-income category ($7,000 to $15,000) earned 9.3 percent less, whereas those in the two highest-parental-income groups earned 10 and 11.9 percent more, respectively.[5] We computed these gaps by estimating a model of earnings that accounts only for parental-income levels and no other explanatory factors.

The next two columns in Tables 7.1 and 7.2 show the earnings gaps once we do take account of several noncurriculum factors. The bottom half of the tables indicate which factors we account for in our model of

---

[3]These earnings deficits are smaller than those reported in other literature because of the characteristics of the HSB data. The HSB dataset has smaller Hispanic gaps than the Census data because the HSB sample includes only those people who are still in school as of the second half of their sophomore year in high school. Thus, it excludes students who drop out of school at an early age, as well as immigrants who had no U.S. education.

[4]The income categories in this chapter are defined in 1980 dollars. To get a better feel for those categories, we list the 1980 dollar amount followed by its 1999 dollar equivalent in parentheses: $7,000 ($14,153), $15,000 ($30,327), $20,000 ($40,437), $25,000 ($50,546), and $38,000 ($76,830).

[5]It is important to note that because these results are derived from a very simple regression model, they are equal to unweighted differences in mean earnings between the different groups of students in the regression sample only. Weighted mean earnings gaps from the regression sample are slightly larger. Unweighted differences in *median* earnings for the regression sample, as opposed to mean earnings, are even larger.

Table 7.2

Percentage Earnings Gap Based on Parental-Income Difference in 1991 Earnings Relative to Students from Middle-Income Families

	(1)	(2)	(3)
<$7K	−25.4**	−15.7**	−11.6**
$7K–$15K	−9.3**	−3.8*	−2.5
$15K–$20K	−2.5	0.2	0.1
$25K–$38K	10.0**	7.3**	7.3**
$38K +	11.9**	5.9**	6.1**
Other controls			
Curriculum	No	No	Yes
Demographic	No	Yes	Yes
Family	No	Yes	Yes
School	No	Yes	Yes

NOTES: The effects of parental income are measured relative to students from families with incomes between $20,000 and $25,000. Column 1 represents a simple model of 1991 annual earnings explained by family income only. There are no other controls in this model. Columns 2 and 3 represent models that control for demographic, family, and school characteristics. The specific variables in each of these categories can be found in Table 5.1. The model in column 3 also controls for curriculum. The change in the effects from column 2 to column 3 represents the portion of the earnings gap that curriculum can explain.

**Significant at the 5 percent level; *significant at the 10 percent level.

earnings. As the second column of Table 7.1 shows, the Hispanic and black earnings gaps disappear entirely in the more realistic model of earnings that accounts for the student's demographic, family, and school characteristics.[6] Asian students still experience an earnings premium relative to white students, but the effect is statistically weak.[7] Native

---

[6]We include all of the demographic, family, and school controls listed in Table 5.1. Although we estimate the gaps to be −1 percent for black students and 1 percent for Hispanic students, these effects are statistically indistinguishable from 0.

[7]It is significant at the 10 percent level.

American students still experience an earnings deficit when considering these other factors. What factors are responsible for most of the closure in the earnings gaps? Either parental income or parental education alone can explain nearly all of the Hispanic gap and about half of the black gap. Together, the two measures of parental background can account for the entire earnings gap between whites and either of these minority groups.

As the second column of Table 7.2 demonstrates, the earnings gaps related to parental income groups are much smaller once we control for demographic, family, and school factors, yet the gaps are still present after accounting for these other characteristics. Students from the lowest-income families earn 15.7 percent less than those from middle-income families, and students from the highest-income families earn 5.9 percent more.

Can math curriculum explain a portion of these gaps that remain once we account for noncurriculum factors? In column 3 of Table 7.1, we show the ethnic earnings gaps that account for the student's high school math courses. Once we control for math curriculum, the remaining Native American earnings deficit and the Asian earnings premium are no longer statistically different from zero. In other words, differences in the type of math courses taken by students of these ethnicities, relative to white students, can explain why they have different earnings than white students. More interesting, controlling for curriculum provides weak evidence that Hispanic students are predicted to earn 3.7 percent more than whites given similar curriculum and background characteristics.[8]

Similarly, column 3 of Table 7.2 shows the earnings gaps related to parental income once we account for curriculum. Math curriculum appears to be responsible for over 25 percent of the unexplained earnings gap experienced by students from lowest-income families relative to middle-income families.[9] The gap becomes insignificant for the next-to-

---

[8]This effect is significant only at the 10 percent level, so it does not meet the requirements for strict statistical significance.

[9]This is computed as the percentage change in the lowest-income (less than $7,000) parental effect from column 2 to column 3 of Table 7.2. If we include measures of

lowest income group ($7,000 to $15,000) after adding curriculum to the model. However, students from the two highest-parental-income categories still experience about the same earnings premium that they do without controlling for curriculum. Thus, curriculum explains a large portion of the earnings gap between students from low-income and middle-income families, but it does not help to explain the gap between students from high-income and middle-income families.[10]

The results from this section carry important policy implications. Whereas many other factors help to determine the labor market success of students whose parents have average and high incomes, students of low-income families could significantly improve their earnings prospects with a better curriculum. Policies aimed at encouraging, motivating, and preparing low-income students to take a more rigorous curriculum could have substantial benefits for both current and future generations.[11]

We repeat this analysis for gender-based subsamples and display the regression results in Appendix Table E.1. We caution that because of the smaller sample sizes of these subgroups, the results may lack precision. However, there are some interesting similarities and differences that deserve mention. For men, there appears to be a statistically significant earnings gap for blacks and a weakly significant earnings gap for Hispanic students in the model that controls for personal, family, and school characteristics but excludes curriculum. Adding curriculum to

English, science, and foreign language curriculum in the model that controls for math, the gap narrows by about another 7 percent.

[10]In this section, we discuss only results from adding the six math curriculum measures. Adding the aggregate number of math credits earned instead of the six separate measures does not induce as much of a change in the ethnic or parental-income effect. This indicates the importance of being able to use disaggregated curriculum information to explain earnings.

[11]The overall picture does not change if we also control for GPA in the column 2 and column 3 models. The parental income gap between the lowest-income and middle-income students shrinks from –0.159 to –0.122 once we account for curriculum, representing a 23 percent drop rather than a 25 percent drop. Once again, the gap between the highest- and middle-parental-income groups does not change from model to model once we control for math curriculum. If we additionally control for the student's highest educational attainment in the column 2 and column 3 models, the lowest- to middle-parental-income earnings gap changes from –0.123 to –0.107 when we add controls for curriculum, representing a 13 percent change, yet the earnings gap between middle- and high-income students does not close.

this model eliminates the Hispanic effect and causes the black-white earnings gap to decrease from 9.4 percent to 8.1 percent.[12] On the other hand, Hispanic and black females experience an earnings premium after controlling for demographic, family, and school characteristics that only increases once curriculum controls are added. The earnings premium experienced by Asians actually decreases once curriculum controls are added. The opposite direction in which ethnic effects work for the genders may explain why the effects are not detectable for the pooled sample of men and women.

The results regarding earnings gaps related to parental-income levels are much more comparable between the genders. Before including the math curriculum measures in the model for either gender, workers from the lowest-parental-income bracket are predicted to earn significantly less than workers in the middle-income ($20,000 to $25,000) comparison group, whereas workers in the two highest-income categories are predicted to earn significantly more. Accounting for curriculum causes the earnings gap between the lowest-income and middle-income families to decline 33 percent for females and 23 percent for males.[13] Curriculum does not change the effect of having high-income parents.

This chapter has asked whether observed differences in earnings related to race, ethnicity, and parental income might in part reflect variations in the high school curriculum taken by students from various backgrounds. For the pooled sample of men and women, earnings models that control for a student's demographic, family, and school characteristics indicate that ethnicity does not affect earnings. Thus, standard background variables can fully account for the gaps in earnings between races, leaving no role for curriculum in explaining earnings gaps. The HSB dataset underrepresents workers who drop out of school or immigrants who have never attended American high schools, which may explain our surprising finding that standard background variables fully

---

[12]Because these numbers represent the regression coefficients in a log-earnings model, they are a first-order approximation to the earnings gap.

[13]Including English, science, and foreign language curriculum in the model that controls for math causes the gaps to narrow by another 4 percent for males and 7 percent for females.

account for ethnic earnings gaps.[14] However, when we repeated the analysis for men and women separately, we found some weak evidence that curriculum helps to explain the lower earnings of Hispanic men relative to white men.

In sharp contrast, the effect that curriculum could play in decreasing the earnings gap related to parental income is quite remarkable.[15] Variations in the standard set of background variables can explain some but not all of the earnings differences related to parental income. Variations in high school curriculum can account for over one-quarter of the remaining earnings gap between students with the lowest parental income and middle-income students. Similarly, the gap between the second-lowest-income group and the middle-income group becomes statistically insignificant after controlling for curriculum. Our findings are especially important because it is most likely the low-income students who slip through the cracks or are diverted into the less-rigorous curriculum paths. The results imply that if policies are in place to target these students and arm them with the prerequisites necessary to succeed in the more rigorous courses, the school system might increase the effectiveness of high school education for disadvantaged students.

---

[14]This dataset especially underrepresents Hispanic dropouts because they are especially likely to leave school before grade 10.

[15]It is important to bear in mind that although we did not explicitly find that standardizing the curriculum can help narrow the ethnic earnings gap, the ethnic composition of students in the lowest-parental-income group is such that narrowing this gap would be a step toward narrowing the ethnic earnings gap as well: 30 percent of the lowest-income students are Hispanic, 20 percent are black, and 34 percent are white.

8. Concluding Remarks

This report has examined the relationship between the curriculum students take in high school and their educational attainment and earnings approximately a decade after graduation. Given past evidence that math achievement is particularly strongly related to the earnings of workers, the report focuses mainly, but not exclusively, on the effect of math courses.

For two reasons, we hypothesized that students who take more math courses in high school might later earn more in the labor market. First, a richer high school curriculum increases the ability of students to gain admission to, and to graduate from, college. We call this the "indirect effect" of curriculum on earnings. Second, a richer high school curriculum may directly increase a person's earnings later in life because it increases the person's cognitive ability and all-around productivity. We consider this the direct effect of curriculum on earnings.

Our graphs and simple correlations establish a strong relation between math curriculum and both the probability of college graduation and earnings 10 years after students graduate from high school. But any reader of this report has good reason to wonder whether such correlations are causal. For instance, suppose that students who grow up in an affluent family tend to receive relatively more encouragement from parents to excel academically and have more academic resources in the home such as books and computers. Such students are more likely not only to take advanced math courses in high school but to graduate from college and to earn high wages in the labor market. In such a case, family income, rather than curriculum, might be the driving force behind higher wages. In another scenario, students may vary in motivation or ability. More able students might not only enroll in a richer set of high school courses but also are likely to earn higher wages later in life. It would be misleading to interpret the positive correlation between curriculum and earnings that would result from such a scenario as being caused by curriculum.

Our statistical analyses of the effect of curriculum on both college graduation and earnings pay close attention to these issues. To minimize the possibility that curriculum is merely standing in for other factors such as family income, parental education, or school resources, the analyses take account of such student and school characteristics. In addition, the analyses use a number of techniques to take account of variations among students in ability and motivation.

Our statistical analyses predict that taking a richer math curriculum in high school does indeed increase both the probability of graduating from college and earnings about a decade after the end of high school. Figure 8.1 shows how the probability of graduating from college is related to the highest math course that students take in high school.[1]

Because earnings provide a better measure of how well off a person is than a simple indicator of whether a person has graduated from college, we now summarize some of the more important findings with respect to earnings. Earnings effects vary with the academic level of the course, with calculus having the largest effects and the lower-level math courses having progressively smaller effects. The most robust finding is simply that "math matters." For instance, in our main models, a number of math courses are significantly related to earnings. Figure 8.2 shows the predicted effect that additional specific math courses have on earnings after accounting for demographic, family, and school characteristics, and it divides this effect up into the direct cognitive effect (the dark bars) and the indirect effect that works through educational attainment (the light bars). Because of the important role that ability and motivation can play in affecting which math courses students take, we treated these confounding factors separately from the others. Figure 8.3 shows the direct math effects from the previous figure both before and after accounting for ability and motivation effects. In another model that uses an "instrumental variables" technique to control for unobserved

---

[1] Here we show the overall results for the average student (i.e., a student with the mean values of all of the explanatory factors in the model), whereas in Chapter 4 we showed the results for particular ethnic and socioeconomic groups.

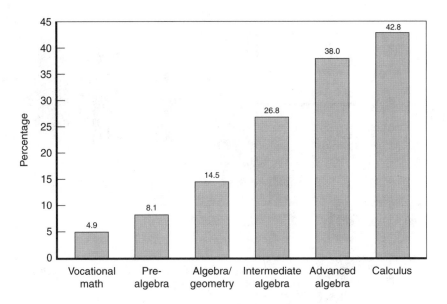

NOTES: When estimating the math effects, we control for the student's demographic, family, and school characteristics as well as the student's ability as measured by his or her math GPA and math test score. The highest completed math course is the highest-level course in which the student completed at least one semester.

Figure 8.1—Predicted Percentage of Students Graduating from College Given Their Highest Completed Math Course

variations in student ability within each school, algebra/geometry credits quite strikingly have the largest predicted effect on earnings, whereas the remaining courses have insignificant effects.

These results persist when we include English, science, and foreign language curriculum measures in the model, although some of these other types of courses appear to influence earnings as well. Nonetheless, math does stand out, more than courses in many other areas, as a subject matter that really seems to make a difference.

The curriculum results emanate from the detailed manner in which we measure curriculum and this is one of the major contributions of this report. If we simply use the aggregate number of credits earned in the separate subjects, the effects of some subjects disappear entirely, whereas the aggregate effect of other subjects represents an average of what the

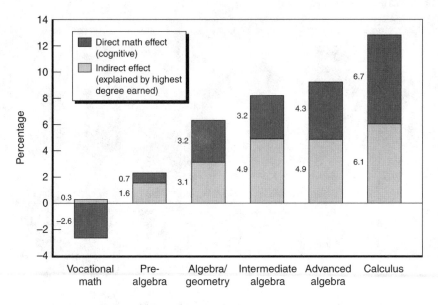

NOTES: When estimating the math effects, we control for the student's demographic, family, and school characteristics. An additional math course refers to an additional year-long course.

Figure 8.2—Predicted Percentage Increase in Earnings Resulting from an Additional Math Course (direct and indirect effects)

detailed curriculum effects would be. In other words, a policy prescription that all students should take more math in high school might not produce the intended consequences. What appears to matter most for increasing both earnings and the probability of graduating from college is that students *progress* beyond basic courses such as vocational math and pre-algebra toward more advanced topics.

The report has also assessed the effect of curriculum on *intergroup* variations in earnings. In addressing this issue, it is important to account first for the possible role of variations in family background in explaining these gaps. Virtually all of the gap in earnings between whites and most minority groups 10 years after graduation from high school can be accounted for by differences in family background and to a lesser extent school characteristics, without any need to control for curriculum at all. In contrast, the earnings gap related to variations in parental-income levels cannot be fully explained by family and school characteristics. We

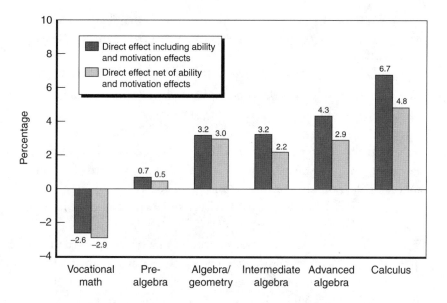

NOTES: When estimating the math effects, we control for the student's demographic, family, and school characteristics. To estimate the effects net of ability and motivation, we also control for the student's math GPA. An additional math course refers to an additional year-long course.

Figure 8.3—Predicted Percentage Increase in Earnings Resulting from an Additional Math Course (direct effects with and without ability and motivation)

did not find that curriculum could explain much of the earnings gap among students from higher-family-income categories. However, curriculum can explain nearly one-quarter of the remaining gap between students in the lowest-income group and students in the middle of five income groups. Perhaps even more striking, math curriculum can account for almost all of the earnings gap between students from the second-lowest and middle-family-income groups.[2] Overall, this finding is an important result because it offers a tool for increasing the degree of equity in students' labor market outcomes later in life.

---

[2]Once again, it is worth noting that the aggregate number of math credits a student earns cannot explain as much of this earnings gap.

To sum up, the main message of this report is that math matters. Math curriculum is strongly related to student outcomes nearly 10 years after students should have graduated from high school. Curriculum has an indirect effect on earnings by affecting who attends and succeeds in college. However, even independent of a student's ultimate level of educational attainment, math is predicted to affect earnings directly, especially for women.

Another important message of this report is that not all math courses are equal. More-advanced math has a much larger predicted effect on college graduation rates and earnings.

At the school and district level, what lessons can be gleaned from our study? The analysis strongly suggests that algebra, beyond the introductory level, acts as a "gateway" course that opens opportunities to high school students in both postsecondary education and the labor market. Thus, our results provide some empirical support for initiatives at the district or school level to increase the percentage of students who complete algebra courses.

We found no evidence that the effectiveness of additional math courses increases in schools with more highly paid teachers, better-educated teachers, or smaller pupil-teacher ratios, although we caution that our conclusions might have changed had a larger dataset been available. For an example of research that suggests different conclusions, see Betts, Rueben, and Danenberg (2000). Their detailed study of California schools at the classroom level presents evidence that the provision of advanced curriculum in the state's high schools is systematically linked to the level of experience and education of teachers. If these finding apply generally, then enriching the curriculum at a given high school might first require investments in improved teacher training to succeed. In addition, interventions in curriculum in middle schools and even elementary schools may need to precede bold initiatives to increase the rigor of the curriculum offered in California's high schools.

There is a second reason why a mandate to reform minimum course requirements could backfire, especially if the reforms were sudden and substantial. It would clearly be a mistake to insist that within a short time period all students must finish courses through, for instance, calculus, while in high school. The large earnings premium we observe in our data for students with advanced math skills reflects the relative scarcity of such workers. A massive increase overnight in the number of workers with such skills would surely decrease the wage premium for such workers, through the simple law of supply and demand. But it does seem likely that improving the math curriculum for the least highly achieving students could materially improve their economic prospects. Further research on these issues is essential.

Our findings are relevant for the many policymakers who have focused on the large gaps in educational achievement among various socioeconomic groups in the state and the nation. Our results here are not definitive, owing to the small size of some of the socioeconomic groups in our sample. Nonetheless, the findings are intriguing: Policies that target low-income students and those who go to schools with a high percentage of disadvantaged students may be particularly well rewarded. We also found some evidence that variations in math curriculum might account for roughly one-quarter of the earnings gap between students from families with the lowest income and middle income. Thus, attempts to enrich the curriculum in schools serving relatively disadvantaged students might provide quite a powerful tool for narrowing the earnings gap between disadvantaged and more-advantaged students.

The finding that more-advanced math courses have larger predicted effects on earnings than do less-advanced courses is of particular relevance to California, which is in the middle of implementing a set of major reforms designed to improve school quality, especially in the schools with lowest achievement. One part of this reform effort involves developing a set of grade-specific content standards in math and other subjects. A second part of the reforms aims to devise a new high school "exit" exam that all students must take before graduating from high school, beginning with students projected to graduate in 2004. In November 1999, Governor Gray Davis strongly recommended to the State Board of Education that it include algebra in the exam. However, in December 1999, the board reached an impasse on the governor's recommendation, in part because state law did not, at that time, make algebra a graduation requirement. Later, in fall 2000, California did pass legislation making algebra a high school requirement. At about the same time, initial results from field tests of the high school exit exam began to suggest that large percentages of California high school students might fail the test, leading to a suggestion that the algebra component of the test be simplified somewhat.

Our results cannot provide a detailed resolution of these policy debates. But our findings indicate that it is the type of math course, especially algebra/geometry courses, that seems to matter most for long-term outcomes. Throughout a battery of robustness tests, credits earned in the algebra/geometry category most reliably remained a statistically significant predictor of earnings.

Policymakers need to monitor the package of school resources that appears to be necessary to provide all students with equal opportunity to take some of the more-advanced math classes in high school. This package includes not only overall spending but also strategies aimed at providing an appropriate foundation for students to succeed in these more-advanced math courses. Subject to this qualification, increasing math requirements for high school graduation in reasonable and methodical ways could do much to improve equality in student outcomes 10 years after high school graduation. In this light, the governor's recent efforts to funnel additional resources to underperforming schools, together with his proposal to include algebra in the formal requirements for high school graduation, hold considerable promise. These reforms maintain public attention on issues such as school spending, class size, and teacher quality, while at the same time bringing new attention to the heart of the matter: what students actually learn in school.

Appendix A
Data Description

As we discussed in Chapter 4, the principal source of data for this report is the High School and Beyond (HSB) Sophomore Cohort: 1980–92 data. This is a longitudinal study of a cohort of students who were high school sophomores in 1980. The most recent follow-up survey of these students was conducted in 1992.

For the purpose of this study, the HSB data are the most timely and detailed data collected by the Department of Education. The other potential candidates are the National Education Longitudinal Study of 1988 (NELS:88) and National Longitudinal Study of the High School Class of 1972 (NLS-72). NELS collects data from a cohort of 1988 eighth graders. Like HSB, it contains detailed transcript data; however, even at the latest follow-up for which data are available, the respondents are too young to include college graduates in a meaningful wage study.[1] NLS-72 collects information for a cohort of 1972 high school seniors and follows them through 1986. Although it does contain wage data and information on college attainment sufficiently long after high school graduation, it suffers from three main shortcomings. It does not contain much information on high school dropouts because most students who drop out do so before their senior year. In addition, its curriculum measures are much less detailed than those found in the HSB data. Finally, it seems worthwhile to update Altonji's results with a group of students who graduated from high school in 1982, a decade later than the NLS-72 cohort.

We constructed data on mathematics curriculum from the high school transcript data.[2] Although a public-use transcript data file is

---

[1]These data may still be suitable to study earnings for a subsample of those with no postsecondary education.

[2]Other academic subject areas are also used, but we describe math here for simplicity.

available, we opted for the more-detailed restricted version. With this data file, every high school math course a student took is classified into 42 categories using the standard Classification of Secondary School Courses (CSSC).[3] Such detail is quite appealing but rather analytically daunting. We reduced these 42 classes into six broader categories based on a classification system provided by the National Center for Education Statistics (NCES).

In the unrestricted version of the data, only the total number of math classes that a student took is available. Thus, no measure of course difficulty is available. Also problematic is that the pre-calculated course counts in the transcript data give each course taken a count of one. So, if one student takes a one-year algebra course and another student takes two one-semester algebra courses, they will have course counts of 1 and 2, respectively. In essence, the two students have taken the same course, but their tally is misleading. This could lead to measurement error bias in our models that would bias the estimated effect of math toward zero. So, we calculate the number of credits students earn directly from the raw transcript data and do not use the pre-calculated version.

The Variables in Our Models

In this section, we document the math and science course classification systems and describe the variables that we use in this report. We report the actual variable names from the HSB dataset in capital letters and describe the slight modifications and improvements that we made to them for use in our analysis.

Math Course Classification System

NCES provided us with the math and science course classification system that they used to construct "pipeline composite variables" for the NELS:88 data.[4] These provided the backbone of our classification

---

[3]The CSSC can be found in Jones (1982).

[4]The authors would like to thank Jeff Owings and Robert Atanda at NCES for providing us with the course classifications.

system, although we did deviate slightly after some initial analysis.[5] We maintain the NCES category titles but also include a brief description of the category in parentheses (see Table A.1). Throughout the report, we refer to the categories by these descriptive titles.

Table A.1

Math Course Classification System

1	Non-academic (vocational math)	General (1 and 2), basic (1, 2, and 3), consumer, technical, vocational, review
2	Low-academic (pre-algebra)	Pre-algebra, algebra 1 (part 1), algebra 1 (part 2), geometry informal
3	Middle academic I (algebra/geometry)	Algebra 1, geometry (plane and solid), unified 1, unified 2
4	Middle academic II (intermediate algebra)	Algebra 2, unified 3
5	Advanced I and II (advanced algebra)	Algebra 3, algebra-trigonometry, analytic geometry, linear algebra, probability, statistics, pre-calculus
6	Advanced III (calculus)	AP calculus, calculus-analytic geometry, calculus

Science Course Classification System

The NCES provided us with three different classification systems for science courses. We merged them into one system of six categories. (See Table A.2.)

Foreign Language Course Classification System

Foreign language is more difficult to disaggregate by level. Generally, students follow a progression of language courses starting with level 1 and finishing with up to level 4 of the same language. In this case, taking more courses indicates taking higher-level courses as well. However, students may also take two years of one language then two

---

[5]The math classification system used by NCES included a separate category for pre-calculus (called Advanced II), but after some initial analysis, we decided to combine it with the Advanced I level.

Table A.2

Science Course Classification System

1	Basic biology	Basic biology
2	General biology, secondary life science	General biology 1, secondary life sciences (ecology, marine biology, zoology, human physiology)
3	Primary physics	Primary physical sciences (applied physical science, earth science, college prep earth science, unified science), general science
4	Secondary physics	Secondary physical sciences (astronomy, environmental science, geology, oceanography, general physics, consumer chemistry, introductory chemistry)
5	Chemistry 1 and physics 1	Chemistry 1, physics 1
6	Chemistry 2, physics 2, advanced placement biology	Chemistry 2, physics 2, advanced placement biology

years of another. It is not clear that one pattern of course-taking is particularly more rigorous than the other and therefore we do not distinguish between the two. However, we do recognize that the third foreign language course a student takes may have a much different effect than the first language class a student takes. Therefore, we converted the total foreign language credits earned into two mutually exclusive variables. One designates whether the student took one or two courses, whereas the other signals that the student took three or four courses.

Other Variables

Earnings. To calculate the log of 1991 earnings, we used the HSB reported 1991 annual earnings: Y4301B9.[6] We checked these data

---

[6]Although the last follow-up took place in the spring of 1992, the annual earnings data from that year seem inaccurate. Whereas the average annual earnings steadily increased from 1982 through 1991 in an expected fashion, they fell to about half of their expected value in 1992, almost as if some respondents gave year-to-date earnings information. Even after discussions with the HSB personnel from the Department of Education, the cause of this is not clear. Although the 1991 earnings reports were self-

extensively to ensure plausible values. We individually inspected all earnings over $75,000 and all earnings that changed by more than $30,000 between 1991 and either the year before or the year after. By comparing the 1991 data to the 1990 and 1992 data, it seemed that a high value was often the result of a data entry error. For example, a common scenario was 1990 earnings of $11,500 that jumped to $115,000 in 1991 and back to $11,500 in 1992. In such obvious cases, we assumed that an extra zero had been inadvertently entered for the 1991 data, and we used $11,500 as the 1991 value. Big changes in earnings were sometimes explained by the fact that a student recently obtained a bachelor's degree and so went from earning nothing to earning $40,000. We left such values untouched. It is important to note that the 1992 data were useful in this exercise but not usable for more-extensive purposes because of their inaccurate nature.

To determine an approximate monthly wage, we divided annual earnings by the number of months that the respondent was employed during 1991. We derived the number of months employed from the HSB variables: Y4302A61–Y4302A72. We excluded the number of months in which the respondent was unemployed and receiving compensation in the measure of "months employed."

Educational Attainment. The HSB data contain two measures of the respondent's highest educational degree obtained by June 1992: HDEG and HGHDG92. We used HGHDG92 as the primary measure of highest degree earned, because it is derived from actual college transcripts as well as interview data. Because HDEG comes only from transcript data, in cases where recent transcript information is missing, HGHDG92 will most likely assign higher levels of education, assuming that the student reports these levels in the interview.

We did make two slight adjustments. First, we created a new category for those students with some postsecondary education but no degree. If a student was a high school graduate (according to HGHDG92) but had some postsecondary education (according to HDEG), he or she was put into this new category. Additionally, if

---

reported and retrospective in nature, they are likely to be accurate because the data were gathered in 1992 (and near tax time for 1991 income).

HGHDG92 was missing, we used HDEG to fill in the gaps. These categories were then used to construct a series of dummy variables indicating the respondent's highest degree obtained.

We believe that students who dropped out of high school but later obtained a high school diploma or GED are included in the "high school graduates" category (or higher if they go on to earn a higher degree). Of the students who received the HSB first follow-up dropout questionnaire in the spring of 1992, 43 percent were classified by the HGHDG92 variable as having a high school diploma or higher.[7]

College Major. Using MAJUG1, we constructed a series of dummy variables representing the major associated with the respondent's earliest bachelor's degree. Only those students who completed at least some postsecondary education were assigned major categories. If the student did not complete a bachelor's degree, but still had a major reported on his or her college transcript, the student was assigned that major. Guided by Grogger and Eide (1995), we divided the 100-plus categories found in MAJUG1 into nine broad categories: (1) business: accounting, finance, operations research, business administration, marketing, data processing and economics; (2) engineering: engineering, computer programming, information sciences, architecture; (3) science and math: physical sciences, life sciences, agricultural sciences, natural resources, mathematics; (4) education and letters: education, letters, philosophy, religious studies, visual and performing arts, foreign languages, English, liberal studies, library sciences; (5) social sciences: social sciences (excluding economics), communications, civics, psychology, public administration, protective services, interdisciplinary studies, area and ethnic studies, law, journalism; (6) technical: construction, mechanics, transportation, design; (7) health: dental and medical technologies, health, nursing, audiology, dentistry, medicine, public health, food sciences; (8) other majors: home economics, cosmetology, recreation; (9) missing majors.

---

[7]To the extent that students who obtained a GED are classified as "high school graduates" in our earnings models, the estimates of having less than a conventional high school diploma will be understated and the estimates of having a degree higher than a conventional high school diploma will be overstated. We thank Richard Murnane for pointing out this issue.

Demographic Characteristics. The composite variables RACE and SEX were used to construct zero-one dummy variables for ethnicity and gender. The age of the respondent was calculated using the birthday-related questions that were asked in the base year as well as in the follow-up surveys. When the birthdays were not the same for the different waves of the survey, we used the earliest birthday. Marital status was calculated using the monthly marital status variables Y4401A97-A99 and Y4401AA0-A8. Students were considered married in 1991 if they were married, in a marriage-like relationship, reunited, or remarried for at least one month in 1991.

Family Characteristics. To form the family income categories, we used the 1980 student-reported family income category BB101. Where this value was missing, we instead used FAMINC, another student-reported family income category obtained after 1980. Because the income categories from these two separate years did not coincide exactly, we condensed them into six income categories that are better aligned. This potentially provides about 2,200 more usable observations for the entire HSB sample of students.

To compute a series of parental educational attainment dummy variables, we used BB039 and BB042. We constructed seven education categories each for the mother and father: less than high school, high school, vocational school, some college, college graduate, advanced degree, and missing.

To determine whether at least one parent was a U.S. native, we used the HSB variables BB040 and BB043.

To determine the number of siblings, we used BB096A-E, FY106-09, and TY5A-M. We used the number of siblings calculated from the 1982 questions. If that was missing, we used the number calculated from the 1986 variables.

School Characteristics. We do not report all of the variables that we used to control for school characteristics, but we do mention modifications that we made to a few of them. After analyzing frequencies of the school variables, we felt that some values should be treated as missing. We generally did this when there was a large discontinuity in values. We set the following variables to missing: books per student if it was greater than 142, student-teacher ratios if they were less than one or greater than 82, length of school year if it was less than 179 or greater than 190, and teacher salary if it was less than $6,000.

Math Test Score. The math test score that we included was based on a math test in which students had 21 minutes to answer 38 questions. The questions required them to compare two quantities and determine whether one was greater, whether they were equal, or whether the relationship was indeterminable based on the given data. We used the HSB-computed Item Response Theory (IRT) scores from this test as our measure of math test score.[8]

Grade Point Average and Number of Credits Earned. We computed the student's math GPA on a scale of 0 to 4.3. We took a weighted average of the student's grade points for each course, where the weights were the number of credits that the student earned for the class. These credits were either 0.25, 0.33, 0.5, or 1, depending on whether the course length was a quarter, trimester, semester, or, more commonly, a year-long course.[9] We converted letter grades to grade points. An "A" received 4 points, a "B" received 3 points, a "C" received 2 points, and a "D" received 1 point. We added 0.3 points for a "plus" and deducted 0.3 points for a "minus." For example, we counted a "B+" as 3.3 points.

If a student failed a course, but subsequently retook it and passed it, we included the letter grade and credit information from the successful completion of the course in the student's GPA, but we ignored the information from the failed attempt. We believed that it is the *final* level of success in a given course that is likely to have the greater effect on a student's subsequent educational attainment and earnings. If, however, the student failed a course and did not repeat it successfully, we included

---

[8]IRT is a "method of estimating achievement level by considering the pattern of right, wrong, and omitted responses on all items administered to an individual student. Rather than merely counting right and wrong responses, the IRT procedure also considers characteristics of each of the test items, such as their difficulty and the likelihood that they could be guessed correctly by low-ability individuals. IRT scores are less likely than simple number-right formula scores to be distorted by correct guesses on difficult items if a student's response vector also contains incorrect answers to easier questions." See Ingels et al. (1995, p. M-4).

[9]This credit measure was standardized, so that a typical one-year course was assigned 1 credit and a half-year course was assigned 0.5 credits. These standardized credits are also known as Carnegie units. They were standardized based on a formula that takes into account the number of minutes per school year that the class meets.

the credit information in the student's GPA calculation but assigned 0 grade points to the course. In other words, we gave the student credit for having taken the course, but lowered the GPA accordingly.

The credit values that we used to compute the GPA also served as our measure of math curriculum. So, for example, a student who took a one-year calculus course had a tally of 1 for that course category. A student who took three semesters worth of a geometry course had a tally of 1.5 for that category. In a few cases, students received a grade of "pass" in a course. We did not include these grades in the GPA calculations but we did add the number of credits earned to the tally of credits earned by the student.

We estimated an alternative specification where we included only the courses that the student passed in the GPA calculation and in the tally of credits that the student earned. The results from our main models did not change when we used this alternative measure.

Data Accuracy

As noted above, we devoted an extensive amount of time to inspecting plausible data values. The values that seemed extremely questionable were treated as missing. For example, we considered student-teacher ratios of 0.17 and of 2,000 to be invalid and assumed them to be missing. For variables other than the dependent variable (college graduation in Chapter 4 and earnings in Chapter 5) and the curriculum measures, we adopted the policy of setting missing values equal to zero and then including a 0-1 dummy variable indicating whether the variable was missing or not. This allowed us to work with a larger sample size.

Missing Observations and Excluded Data

In this section, we document how the HSB sample of 14,825 observations shrank to the 5,919 observations that we used for the earnings regression analysis. Not only did we lose observations because data are missing for crucial variables, but we also placed a restriction on the nonmissing earnings data that excluded certain observations.

In our analysis, we wanted to avoid several selection problems inherent in analyzing the public-private school choice. Therefore, we excluded students from private schools. We also eliminated students who transferred schools while attending high school. Because we believe that school characteristics play an important role in determining student success, we controlled for school characteristics in our regressions; and in the case of students who attended two schools, it was not clear what set of school characteristics to use. Finally, we excluded those students who were enrolled in postsecondary education at any time during 1991 or for whom enrollment data were missing, because their earnings might not be truly reflective of their potential earnings nor of their human capital formation or final signal.[10]

Table A.3 shows how the sample was reduced when we eliminated observations in a specific order. The number and percentage of observations lost is calculated relative to the remaining tally of observations that accounts for all previously listed missing observations and restrictions.

For example, 21 percent of students in the HSB data attended private schools and therefore were excluded from the analysis. Of the remaining public school observations, only 9,116 have nonmissing earnings data. We lost 13.6 of the nonmissing public school observations because of the restriction that earnings must be between $2,000 and $75,000. Only 28 of those observations were lost because of the upper limit that we impose to exclude outliers and inaccurate data.

Table A.4 reports the missing variables in a slightly different format. Rather than computing the number of missing/unusable observations relative to those remaining after other restrictions have been made, this table documents the number and percentage of observations that are missing from the overall sample of public schools. Whereas Table A.3 shows that 11 percent of public school students with nonmissing earnings data in the proper range are missing math curriculum data, Table A.4 shows that 13.6 percent of all public school students are missing curriculum data. Similarly, whereas only 7 percent of those observations with valid earnings and curriculum data are missing the college

---

[10]There were no school attendance data for August 1991, so in practice the restriction applies to those enrolled, or missing enrollment data, during the remaining 11 months of the year.

Table A.3

Number of Additional Missing Observations As More Restrictions Are Enacted

Remaining Observations Tally		Lost Observations Relative to Most Recent Tally	
Total observations in HSB data	14,825		
		−3,101	Lose 21 percent of total sample because some students attend private schools.
Public school observations	11,724		
		−2,608	Lose 22 percent of public school sample because of missing earnings data.
With nonmissing earnings data	9,116		
		−1,208	Lose 13 percent of nonmissing earnings data because earnings are less than $2,000.
		−28	Lose 0.3 percent of nonmissing earnings data because earnings are greater than $75,000.
Between $2,000 and $75,000	7,880		
		−896	Lose 11 percent of valid earnings data because of missing curriculum data.
With valid curriculum data	6,984		
		−418	Lose 6 percent of those with valid earnings and curriculum data because they transferred schools.
		−219	Lose 3 percent of those with valid earnings and curriculum data because they are enrolled in 1991.
		−460	Lose 7 percent of those with valid earnings data because they have missing 1991 enrollment data.
		36	Must add back 36 observations so that we do not double-count those who transferred schools *and* are either enrolled or missing enrollment data.
		−4	Lose 4 observations because of missing age data.
Observations remaining for analysis	5,919		

NOTES: This table documents how the 14,825 observations in HSB are reduced to 5,919 usable regression observations. The right-hand column records the number of omitted observations for each given reason and the left hand column keeps a running tally of the remaining observations after each loss. The number and percentage of observations lost are calculated relative to the most recent tally.

Table A.4

Missing Observations Out of 11,724 Total Public School Observations

Type of Missing Observations	Number of Missing Observations	Missing Observations out of 11,724 (percent)
Missing earnings data	2,608	22.2
Out-of-range earnings data	1,236	10.5
Missing curriculum data	1,591	13.6
Transfer students	949	8.1
Students enrolled in postsecondary education	304	2.6
Missing enrollment data	2,426	20.7
Transfers *and* invalid enrollment (enrolled or missing)	255	2.2

NOTES: This table documents the number and percentage of missing values for some key variables in the analysis. Unlike the previous table, the number of missing values in this table is always calculated relative to the total number (11,724) of public school observations.

enrollment status (Table A.3), nearly 21 percent of all public school students are missing enrollment status. Such comparisons help to demonstrate the overlap between missing earnings data and other missing variables. Clearly, large portions of students who are missing earnings data are also missing enrollment data. In the summary statistics section of Appendix C, we discuss the tests that we perform to help assure us that, despite the loss of observations, the regression sample is representative of the entire sample.

Appendix B

Probit Results

Because there are only two possible outcomes—the student either earns a bachelor's degree or does not—we base our analysis on the following probit model in which we treat the probability of completing college as a nonlinear function of several factors. The model for student i at schools s is:

$$P(college_{is}) = F(X_{is}\beta)$$

where $F(.)$ is the standard normal cumulative distribution function (CDF) and

$$X_{is}\beta = \alpha + \lambda Curric_{is} + \rho_i GPA_{is} +$$
$$\rho_2 TS_{is} + \beta_1 Demo_{is} + \beta_2 Fam_{is} + \beta_3 Sch_{is}$$

where $Curric_{is}$ denotes curriculum, GPA_{is} is math grade point average, TS_{is} is the math test score, $Demo_{is}$ refers to demographic information, Fam_{is} and Sch_{is} are family and school characteristics, respectively. The explanatory variables are described in the main chapter. The vector β represents the coefficients obtained from the maximum likelihood estimation of the probit model. Because of the model's nonlinear nature, the values of β do not represent the marginal effect of a particular explanatory variable on the predicted probability of completing college. So, in addition to presenting the exact probit estimates, we devote a section to interpreting the meaning of the coefficient values and how changes in math curriculum translate into changes in the predicted probability of completing college.

The estimated probit coefficients are given in Table B.1, where each column represents a slightly different model. Our main focus, and the model from which Figures 4.1 and 4.2 are derived, revolves around the model in column 2. This model uses a pooled sample of males and females and controls for aptitude and motivation by including both the

Table B.1

Probit Regression Coefficients from Models of College Completion
(dependent variable = 1 if student graduated from college)

	Pooled (1)	Pooled (2)	Pooled (3)	Male (4)	Female (5)
Pre-algebra	0.259**	0.256*	0.124	0.091	0.422**
	(0.129)	(0.145)	(0.166)	(0.205)	(0.219)
Algebra/geometry	0.706**	0.596**	0.438**	0.553**	0.668**
	(0.087)	(0.102)	(0.118)	(0.134)	(0.166)
Intermediate algebra	1.213**	1.035**	0.822**	1.042**	1.059**
	(0.089)	(0.106)	(0.121)	(0.140)	(0.171)
Advanced algebra	1.583**	1.347**	1.090**	1.342**	1.408**
	(0.089)	(0.108)	(0.123)	(0.143)	(0.173)
Calculus	1.811**	1.472**	1.218**	1.239**	1.917**
	(0.123)	(0.144)	(0.159)	(0.191)	(0.236)
Native American	−0.470**	−0.434*	−0.542**	−0.337	−0.602
	(0.215)	(0.235)	(0.247)	(0.313)	(0.376)
Asian	0.243*	0.210	0.246	0.316	0.065
	(0.128)	(0.146)	(0.155)	(0.204)	(0.216)
Hispanic	−0.121*	−0.022	−0.028	0.039	−0.077
	(0.072)	(0.079)	(0.087)	(0.104)	(0.125)
Black	0.150*	0.280**	0.213**	0.282**	0.287**
	(0.078)	(0.086)	(0.093)	(0.123)	(0.126)
Male	−0.077*	−0.098**	−0.031	N/A	N/A
	(0.044)	(0.048)	(0.052)		
Math GPA	0.370**	0.305**	0.302**	0.360**	0.272**
	(0.028)	(0.032)	(0.034)	(0.045)	(0.046)
Math test score		0.024 **	0.021**	0.018**	0.030**
		(0.003)	(0.004)	(0.005)	(0.005)
Sample	All	All	HS+, BA+	All males	All females
No. of observations	5,827	5,062	3,375	2,678	2,384
Log likelihood	−2,223	−1,944	−1,684	−984	−925

NOTES: Standard errors are in parentheses. Math effects are measured relative to the effect of vocational math being the student's highest course. The highest course is the highest-level course in which the student earned 0.5 Carnegie units or more. Each model controls for demographic, family, and school traits. See Table 4.1 for a complete list. Columns 1–3 use the pooled sample of males and females. Column 3 uses a subsample of college-bound high school students. We exclude those students who have taken no math courses (approximately 18 observations).

**Significant at the 5 percent level; *significant at the 10 percent level.

math GPA and the student's 1980 math IRT test score.[1] For the sake of comparison, we also present model 1, which includes only math GPA for such a control. Both models also control for the standard demographic, family, and school characteristics. Because the curriculum measures are a series of dummy variables, we omit the lowest-level math category (vocational math) as the control group. The remaining math coefficients are measured relative to this omitted group.[2] In both cases, all of the math curriculum measures are significantly different from the effect of the omitted vocational math category. As expected, the math coefficients are positive and increase in magnitude as the difficulty level of the math courses increases. This indicates that taking a more-advanced math course increases the likelihood of graduating from college.[3] In addition to similar trends, models 1 and 2 also yield roughly similar curriculum coefficient values.

To ensure that taking a more advanced math curriculum leads to a higher likelihood of graduating and not just a higher likelihood of attending college, we also estimate the probit model on a restricted sample of those students who obtained some positive amount of postsecondary education. Even for this subsample of college-bound students, a more-advanced math curriculum increases the predicted

---

[1]We limit the sample to those students who have taken at least one math course. This simplifies the analysis and does not substantially change the results.

[2]The curriculum measures that we use in this model are a series of six dummy variables indicating the highest level of math course the student completed during high school. We chose this measure of curriculum, rather than the number of credits earned, to more easily analyze the ensuing probit results.

[3]To verify that succeeding math-level coefficients are significantly different from each other (and not just significantly different from the omitted group), we used a series of likelihood ratio tests. We computed the likelihood ratio statistic based on the log likelihood values from the unrestricted model and a series of restricted models. The LR Test Stat = −2(LogL(restricted) − LogL(unrestricted)). The six restrictions that we tested separately are the effect of math level j equals the effect of math level (j+1) for j = 1 to 5 and a joint test that all of the math levels are equal. We rejected the null at less than the 5 percent level regardless of whether we controlled for GPA alone or GPA and math test score, with one exception. In the model that controlled for both GPA and math test score, we could not reject the hypothesis that the effects of advanced algebra and calculus are the same.

probability of graduating. The coefficients are presented in the third column of Table B.1.

The last variation of the model we estimate is simply the model from column 2 broken down by gender (see columns 4 and 5). The same increasing trend in curriculum coefficients is present in these models. The magnitudes of the curriculum coefficients in each of these subsamples are extremely similar to each other and to the coefficient values of the pooled regression, the most dramatic differences being that calculus and pre-algebra have a much larger effect on the predicted probability of graduation for females than they do for males.

The last item that warrants attention at this stage is the relative importance of GPA with respect to math curriculum. The average GPA for the overall pooled sample is 2.18 (slightly better than a straight "C"). According to model 2, an increase of an entire grade point (to a "B" average) would add only 0.31 units to the $X\beta$ term of the average student. This is about the same increase that occurs if the student completes advanced algebra rather than just stopping at intermediate algebra. Below this level of math course, additional math levels have a much greater effect than a full grade increase in GPA. This indicates that students deciding whether to trade off taking a difficult math course for a boost in their GPA should forgo the course only if by doing so they can raise their GPA by at *least* one full grade. On this same subject, the math test score has a smaller effect compared to any of the math curriculum measures but is still in the same "ballpark." The mean math test score is approximately 13 points. An increase of 10 points (just over one standard deviation) is predicted to cause a 0.24 rise in the $X\beta$ term.

As we mentioned above, the drawback of this genre of nonlinear model is that coefficients *cannot* be interpreted as the marginal effect on the probability of a successful outcome. Because the predicted probability of graduating from college is not equal to $X\beta$ itself, but rather to the normal CDF evaluated at $X\beta$, the change in the predicted probability is the *slope* of the normal CDF evaluated at $X\beta$ (i.e., the standard normal probability distribution function multiplied by β). Because the normal CDF is nonlinear, the slope varies as $X\beta$ varies. To see how, we include a graph of the normal CDF in Figure B.1. At high negative and positive levels of $X\beta$, an increase in $X\beta$ (for example,

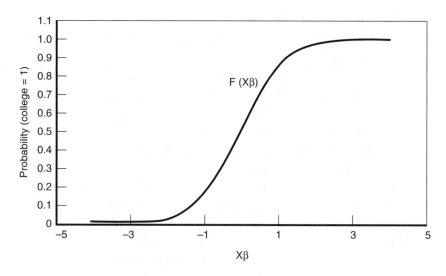

Figure B.1—General Probit Graph

resulting from taking a higher level of math course) causes only a very small change in the predicted probability of graduating from college. However, if Xβ is close to zero before the change occurs, a slight increase in Xβ will have a much larger increase in the predicted probability.

The question then becomes: To calculate the effect that a change in Xβ has on the predicted probability of graduating from college, from what initial value of Xβ should we begin? As we pointed out in Chapter 4, we are interested in how the effects of curriculum vary by ethnicity and socioeconomic groups. Therefore, we divide our sample into 16 subgroups based on four ethnic groups and four parental-income groups. For each subgroup, we calculate the mean values of all of the family, school, and demographic explanatory factors of that group and use this value as our starting point for Xβ.[4] Next, using model 2, we compute F(Xβ), which gives us the baseline predicted probability that the average student within that group graduates from college, given that the highest math class he or she took was vocational math. We then add the pre-algebra coefficient to Xβ and recalculate F(Xβ) to compute the predicted probability that a student graduates from college given that he or she

---

[4]This is the original XB with all of the curriculum measures set to zero.

took up to pre-algebra. We repeat this process for the algebra/geometry through calculus coefficients, each time adding the coefficient of interest to the baseline $X\beta$ value.[5] This yields a range of probabilities describing the likelihood of graduating from college given the six different levels of math courses. Table B.2 presents the predicted probabilities of graduation for the overall group as well as for each of the subgroups. These values were used for the graphs in Figures 4.1 and 4.2.

It is worth mentioning that we also estimated a linear probability model rather than a probit model and found that the math effects on the probability of graduation were in the same ballpark as our exercise predicts. Furthermore, with the linear probability model, we used the same instrumental variables technique that we used in the models of earnings later in the report to net out the ability/motivation effects that might be combined with the math effects. Although the effects of math diminished slightly, the effects of all math courses were still quite strong and very dependent on the level of the math course.

---

[5]Note that normally the product of the explanatory variable and its coefficient should be added to the original XB term. However, because our explanatory variables are 0-1 dummy variables, this reduces to adding the coefficient on its own.

Table B.2

Predicted Probabilities of College Graduation for the Average Person with at Least 0.5 Credits in the Stated Highest Math Course

		Vocational Math	Pre-Algebra	Algebra/ Geometry	Intermediate Algebra	Advanced Algebra	Calculus
Overall	5,104	0.049	0.081	0.145	0.268	0.380	0.428
White, poor income	139	0.016	0.029	0.060	0.133	0.211	0.249
White, low income	1,502	0.049	0.081	0.146	0.269	0.380	0.428
White, medium income	627	0.076	0.120	0.202	0.347	0.467	0.517
White, high income	920	0.104	0.157	0.253	0.411	0.534	0.583
Black, poor income	71	0.022	0.040	0.079	0.165	0.253	0.295
Black, low income	281	0.046	0.077	0.139	0.259	0.369	0.417
Black, medium income	76	0.067	0.107	0.183	0.321	0.439	0.489
Black, high income	80	0.108	0.163	0.260	0.419	0.543	0.592
Hispanic, poor income	133	0.008	0.016	0.035	0.085	0.144	0.174
Hispanic, low income	538	0.023	0.041	0.081	0.169	0.259	0.301
Hispanic, medium income	145	0.035	0.060	0.112	0.219	0.321	0.368
Hispanic, high income	157	0.045	0.075	0.136	0.255	0.364	0.412
Asian, poor income	9	0.034	0.058	0.110	0.215	0.316	0.362
Asian, low income	81	0.083	0.129	0.215	0.363	0.484	0.534
Asian, medium income	20	0.130	0.193	0.299	0.465	0.588	0.636
Asian, high income	34	0.314	0.410	0.545	0.709	0.806	0.838

Table B.2 (continued)

		Vocational Math	Pre-Algebra	Algebra/ Geometry	Intermediate Algebra	Advanced Algebra	Calculus
White, father low education	1,987	0.046	0.076	0.138	0.257	0.367	0.415
White, father high education	580	0.227	0.311	0.439	0.612	0.725	0.765
Black, father low education	227	0.048	0.080	0.144	0.266	0.377	0.425
Black, father high education	39	0.277	0.369	0.502	0.671	0.775	0.811
Hispanic, father low education	605	0.020	0.035	0.071	0.152	0.237	0.277
Hispanic, father high education	85	0.164	0.235	0.351	0.522	0.643	0.689
Asian, father low education	66	0.054	0.089	0.157	0.285	0.398	0.447
Asian, father high education	37	0.412	0.514	0.646	0.792	0.870	0.894

NOTES: The overall sample size is greater than in the probit results because we can include those students who have missing information about their highest degree attained for this exercise. The average person is assumed to have the average values of each of the explanatory variables. These probabilities are calculated using the model that controls for both math GPA and math test score in addition to the standard background characteristics.

Appendix C

Econometric Earnings Models and Results

Econometric Model of Log-Earnings

The standard log earnings model provides the backbone of our analysis.[1] We construct the following linear model of the log of 1991 annual earnings for student i at school s:

$$\ln w_{is} = \alpha + \lambda Curric_{is} + \beta_1 Demo_{is} + \beta_2 Fam_{is} + \beta_3 Sch_{is} + \beta_4 HiDeg_{is} + \varepsilon_{is} \tag{1}$$

where $Curric_{is}$ denotes curriculum, $Demo_{is}$ refers to demographic information, Fam_{is} and Sch_{is} are family and school characteristics, respectively, $HiDeg_{is}$ stands for the highest educational degree obtained by the student, and ε_{is} is an i.i.d. error term.

As we explained in Chapter 5, the main measure of curriculum that we use, $Curric_{is}$, is a vector of the credits earned in each of six math course categories. It then follows that each element in the vector of coefficients, λ, describes the effect of an additional credit in the corresponding math course on the log of earnings.

---

[1] We model the log of earnings rather than the absolute level of earnings for several reasons. For one, it allows us to interpret the regression estimates as the percentage change in earnings resulting from a one-unit change in a particular explanatory factor. This is more appealing than estimates that measure an additive effect (a change in the actual level of earnings), because many of the factors are likely to have a proportionate effect. For example, if we model actual earnings (rather than log of earnings) and find that an additional math course leads to a $2,000 increase in earnings, this means that for workers earning $40,000 annually, that math course has a 5 percent effect, but for a worker earning $5,000 per year, the effect is 40 percent. A model that predicts that increasing the math curriculum will lead to a 5 percent gain in earnings regardless of initial level is arguably more realistic. A second reason why it has become standard practice to model log wages rather than actual wages is that doing so reduces the chance that a few outlier observations skew the regression results.

Although the main body of Chapter 5 lists the variables within the Demo, Fam, Sch, and HiDeg categories, a few technical points deserve mention. Because many of the variables are categorical, we omit one of the categories and represent the remainder by a series of 0–1 dummy variables. Thus, the coefficients on the remaining variables are measured relative to the excluded group. The category breakdowns are explicitly listed in the table of means (Table C.1). Because we include the school variables upon which the HSB survey was stratified, we do not weight the regressions.

As we mentioned in Chapter 5, earnings data do not explicitly measure an hourly wage and so really represent two different effects: a productivity effect and an hours-worked effect. In addition to restricting the income range to help eliminate the hours-worked effect by removing unemployed people from our sample, as a second solution, we estimate a model in which the dependent variable is a monthly wage (calculated as 1991 annual earnings divided by the number of months that the respondent was employed during 1991). We did this to help elicit productivity rather than variations related to labor force attachment, but found that the results changed very little.

In addition to the problem of omitted ability bias mentioned in Chapter 5, we should note the source of another potential model misspecification. In our initial analyses, we assume that the error term is independent across students. However, there could potentially be some shocks that affect all students at a particular school in the same way. In this case, the error term would be correlated across observations from the same school, and OLS would no longer yield efficient estimates of the coefficients. A random effects model takes account of the correlated error terms, yet it turns out that in this case, the random effects estimates are nearly identical to the OLS estimates. So, in this report we present only the OLS results for simplicity. An alternative to the random effects model is a fixed effects model in which we include a dummy variable for each school. We discuss the results from these models in the instrumental variables section of this appendix.

Table C.1

Summary Statistics

	HSB Public School		Regression Sample	
	Unweighted	Weighted	Unweighted	Weighted
Annual 1991 earnings, $	19,168	19,092	22,288	22,077
	(13,532)	(13,534)	(10,954)	(10,929)
Log of 1991 earnings	9.755	9.757	9.872	9.860
	(0.790)	(0.782)	(0.574)	(0.580)
Math curriculum measures				
Credits in vocational math	0.758	0.757	0.685	0.708
	(0.912)	(0.932)	(0.887)	(0.904)
Credits in pre-algebra	0.258	0.262	0.261	0.262
	(0.541)	(0.552)	(0.543)	(0.546)
Credits in algebra/geometry	0.908	0.917	0.988	0.945
	(0.874)	(0.877)	(0.881)	(0.865)
Credits in intermediate algebra	0.265	0.266	0.294	0.279
	(0.461)	(0.470)	(0.476)	(0.469)
Credits in advanced algebra	0.223	0.212	0.250	0.228
	(0.524)	(0.514)	(0.543)	(0.522)
Credits in calculus	0.042	0.039	0.045	0.039
	(0.220)	(0.212)	(0.225)	(0.209)
Demographic characteristics				
Ethnicity = white	0.572	0.702	0.625	0.734
	(0.495)	(0.457)	(0.484)	(0.442)
Ethnicity = Hispanic	0.223	0.131	0.210	0.125
	(0.416)	(0.337)	(0.407)	(0.331)
Ethnicity = black	0.136	0.128	0.110	0.111
	(0.343)	(0.334)	(0.312)	(0.314)
Ethnicity = Asian	0.032	0.012	0.031	0.011
	(0.176)	(0.108)	(0.174)	(0.105)
Ethnicity = Native American	0.023	0.012	0.019	0.011
	(0.151)	(0.109)	(0.137)	(0.106)
Ethnicity = other	0.014	0.015	0.005	0.008
	(0.119)	(0.122)	(0.070)	(0.086)
Male	0.507	0.497	0.539	0.543
	(0.500)	(0.500)	(0.498)	(0.498)
Age as of 6/15/91	27.333	27.297	27.278	27.272
	(0.623)	(0.569)	(0.570)	(0.545)

Table C.1 (continued)

	HSB Public School		Regression Sample	
	Unweighted	Weighted	Unweighted	Weighted
Married in 1991	0.549	0.555	0.562	0.564
	(0.498)	(0.497)	(0.496)	(0.496)
Marital status missing	0.155	0.006	0.005	0.008
	(0.362)	(0.079)	(0.073)	(0.087)
Family characteristics				
Family income: <$7K	0.095	0.075	0.076	0.064
	(0.293)	(0.263)	(0.265)	(0.244)
Family income: $7K–$15K	0.280	0.261	0.282	0.259
	(0.449)	(0.439)	(0.450)	(0.438)
Family income: $15K–$20K	0.168	0.170	0.183	0.179
	(0.374)	(0.376)	(0.387)	(0.383)
Family income: $20K–$25K	0.145	0.148	0.165	0.164
	(0.352)	(0.355)	(0.371)	(0.370)
Family income: $25K–$38K	0.129	0.145	0.147	0.164
	(0.335)	(0.352)	(0.354)	(0.370)
Family income: $38K and up	0.087	0.092	0.092	0.092
	(0.282)	(0.289)	(0.289)	(0.289)
Family income: missing	0.096	0.110	0.055	0.079
	(0.294)	(0.312)	(0.228)	(0.270)
At least one parent U.S. native	0.777	0.785	0.818	0.820
	(0.416)	(0.411)	(0.386)	(0.384)
Native value missing	0.118	0.156	0.089	0.127
	(0.323)	(0.363)	(0.285)	(0.333)
Education of mother: < high school graduate	0.175	0.142	0.168	0.139
	(0.380)	(0.349)	(0.374)	(0.346)
Education of mother: vocational	0.062	0.065	0.068	0.069
	(0.241)	(0.246)	(0.251)	(0.254)
Education of mother: some college	0.087	0.088	0.093	0.090
	(0.282)	(0.283)	(0.290)	(0.287)
Education of mother: college graduate	0.054	0.056	0.065	0.063
	(0.227)	(0.230)	(0.246)	(0.242)
Education of mother: master's, Ph.D.	0.030	0.031	0.032	0.032
	(0.171)	(0.173)	(0.177)	(0.175)
Education of mother: missing	0.282	0.300	0.241	0.262
	(0.450)	(0.458)	(0.427)	(0.440)

Table C.1 (continued)

	HSB Public School		Regression Sample	
	Unweighted	Weighted	Unweighted	Weighted
Education of father: < high school graduate	0.174 (0.379)	0.152 (0.359)	0.174 (0.379)	0.148 (0.355)
Education of father: vocational	0.061 (0.239)	0.060 (0.238)	0.066 (0.249)	0.065 (0.247)
Education of father: some college	0.072 (0.258)	0.076 (0.265)	0.079 (0.270)	0.081 (0.273)
Education of father: college graduate	0.063 (0.243)	0.069 (0.253)	0.074 (0.262)	0.076 (0.265)
Education of father: master's, Ph.D.	0.053 (0.223)	0.054 (0.225)	0.060 (0.238)	0.058 (0.233)
Education of father: missing	0.378 (0.485)	0.386 (0.487)	0.328 (0.470)	0.347 (0.476)
Number of siblings	3.060 (1.792)	2.980 (1.779)	2.964 (1.757)	2.900 (1.766)
Number of siblings missing	0.032 (0.176)	0.016 (0.125)	0.011 (0.106)	0.011 (0.105)
School characteristics				
Urban	0.254 (0.436)	0.219 (0.413)	0.222 (0.416)	0.201 (0.400)
Suburban	0.452 (0.498)	0.464 (0.499)	0.459 (0.498)	0.464 (0.499)
Rural	0.294 (0.456)	0.317 (0.465)	0.319 (0.466)	0.335 (0.472)
Teachers unionized	0.842 (0.365)	0.834 (0.372)	0.846 (0.361)	0.840 (0.367)
Union status missing	0.024 (0.153)	0.020 (0.138)	0.021 (0.144)	0.018 (0.132)
Regular public high school	0.841 (0.365)	0.955 (0.207)	0.859 (0.348)	0.961 (0.194)
Alternative high school	0.035 (0.185)	0.009 (0.094)	0.024 (0.152)	0.007 (0.085)
Cuban Hispanic public school	0.017 (0.131)	0.005 (0.070)	0.013 (0.115)	0.003 (0.057)
Other Hispanic public school	0.106 (0.308)	0.031 (0.173)	0.104 (0.306)	0.029 (0.167)

Table C.1 (continued)

	HSB Public School		Regression Sample	
	Unweighted	Weighted	Unweighted	Weighted
Student teacher ratio	19.432	19.242	19.392	19.243
	(4.598)	(4.581)	(4.634)	(4.536)
High school membership	1,434	1,383	1,404	1,369
	(818)	(793)	(800)	(788)
% disadvantaged students	20.0	16.9	17.9	15.6
	(23.2)	(20.4)	(20.9)	(18.4)
% teachers with master's degree	48.4	48.6	48.2	48.9
	(24.3)	(23.7)	(24.1)	(23.6)
District average spending/ pupil, $	1,588	1,598	1,578	1,602
	(670)	(655)	(669)	(649)
Teacher's salary, $	10,703	10,659	10,691	10,665
	(1,209)	(1,128)	(1,223)	(1,107)
Books per pupil	13.14	13.34	13.68	13.63
	(9.83)	(9.52)	(10.39)	(9.66)
Days in school year	179.8	180	179.8	180.1
	(3.1)	(3.1)	(3.2)	(3.1)
Educational attainment				
Higher than bachelor's degree	0.029	0.031	0.032	0.030
	(0.168)	(0.173)	(0.175)	(0.170)
Bachelor's degree	0.166	0.177	0.222	0.210
	(0.372)	(0.382)	(0.416)	(0.408)
Associate's degree	0.070	0.078	0.085	0.084
	(0.255)	(0.268)	(0.279)	(0.277)
Certificate	0.090	0.110	0.102	0.109
	(0.287)	(0.313)	(0.303)	(0.312)
Some postsecondary education but no degree	0.187	0.190	0.202	0.191
	(0.390)	(0.392)	(0.402)	(0.393)
High school diploma	0.261	0.337	0.297	0.320
	(0.439)	(0.473)	(0.457)	(0.466)
Less than high school	0.060	0.061	0.051	0.049
	(0.238)	(0.239)	(0.219)	(0.215)
Degree missing	0.137	0.015	0.009	0.008
	(0.344)	(0.122)	(0.092)	(0.088)
Additional controls				
Math GPA	2.075	2.096	2.164	2.139
	(0.962)	(0.933)	(0.934)	(0.919)

Table C.1 (continued)

	HSB Public School		Regression Sample	
	Unweighted	Weighted	Unweighted	Weighted
Math IRT test score	11.778	12.249	13.184	12.893
	(9.823)	(9.736)	(9.726)	(9.679)
No. of observations	11,724	11,724	5,919	5,919

NOTES: Standard deviations are in parentheses. Means are calculated before missing values are set to zero. The number of observations represents the maximum possible. Some variables may have fewer observations if there are any missing values. We use the fourth follow-up weight (fu4wt) for the weighted results. The "regression" sample refers to the sample used in the first series of regressions from Chapter 5.

Summary Statistics

Because HSB used a stratified national probability sample of schools in which schools with high percentages of Hispanic students were oversampled, the summary statistics must be weighted to make meaningful projections to the population as a whole.[2] We present both weighted and unweighted means and standard deviations in Table C.1 for both the regression sample and the total sample of public schools. For reasons cited in Chapter 5, we limit the observations used in these calculations to the 11,724 students in public schools.

As expected, because of the oversampling method, the percentage of Hispanics falls dramatically, from 22 percent to 13 percent, when we weight the means (see the change from column 1 to 2 and from column 3 to 4). The rest of the means are extremely similar between the unweighted and weighted versions (for both the total sample and the regression sample).

Appendix A details the loss of observations resulting from missing values for earnings and other variables.[3] Earnings data are missing for approximately 20 percent of the public school sample, primarily because

---

[2]Although that type of school was oversampled, within the school 36 students were randomly selected. Because of the ethnic composition of the oversampled schools, this still leads to a higher than nationally representative proportion of Hispanics in the sample.

[3]Primarily, we drop observations if earnings or curriculum data are missing. We also drop observations of students who transferred schools, who were enrolled in college in 1991, or whose income did not fall in the specified range.

of the lack of participation in the final follow-up. Because some crucial data are missing and therefore unusable in the regression analysis, we also calculate descriptive statistics for the subsample that we use to estimate the earnings models (the regression sample). These are displayed in columns 3 and 4 of the same table. In this subsample, the means and standard deviations are strikingly similar to those obtained when using the full set of potential public school observations.[4] This offers some assurance that sample attrition and missing values have not distorted our sample.

Despite the comparable means between the regression sample and the full sample, we were still concerned that the estimated curriculum effects might not be representative of the entire sample because of the high percentage of students with missing data. As an additional test, we examined whether the relationship between the curriculum variables and the remaining explanatory variables in the earnings model is the same for students in and out of the regression subsample. But rather than compare the simple correlations between the math curriculum variables and the remaining explanatory variables for students in and out of the regression sample, we took a more comprehensive approach.[5] We regressed each of the math credit measures on the remaining explanatory variables, a dummy variable indicating whether the observation is in the regression sample and a series of interaction terms in which each explanatory variable is interacted with that newly constructed dummy variable. Table C.2 shows the number of significant interaction terms that we found from this procedure. In four of the six models, none of the interaction terms were significant. In the vocational math model, only four of the 53 possible interaction terms were significant; and in the algebra model, only one interaction term was significant. Such a small

---

[4]The biggest mean difference occurs in the percentage of sample members who are male. This percentage is 4.5 points higher in the usable regression sample, indicating that we lose a disproportionate number of females. This is not surprising because, on average, more females will be out of the labor force and therefore missing earnings data in the appropriate range.

[5]These explanatory variables include all of the demographic, family, and school characteristics that we described in Chapter 5, as well as the highest educational attainment dummy variables. See Table 5.1 for a complete list of the variables.

Table C.2

Number of Significant Interaction Terms in Tests of Similarity Between the Regression Sample and the Entire Sample

	Number (53 possible per regression)
Vocational math	4
Pre-algebra	0
Algebra/geometry	1
Intermediate algebra	0
Advanced algebra	0
Calculus	0

NOTES: We do not include interaction terms where the variable interacted with the in-regression dummy variable is itself a dummy variable indicating missing data. We fail to reject the hypothesis that the coefficients of the interaction terms are jointly zero for all models except the vocational math and algebra/geometry categories.

number of significant interaction terms gives us reasonable assurances that the relationship between the explanatory factors in the regression model is representative of the entire sample.

Earnings Model Results

Table C.3 shows the complete regression coefficients and standard errors for model (1). In addition, it shows the regression results for the sequence of models discussed in Chapter 5.

Alternative Curriculum Measurement

As an alternative to using the number of credits earned in each level of math class as the measure of curriculum, we constructed a series of dummy variables indicating the highest level of math course the student attained. The coefficient values on these dummy variables were virtually identical to the appropriate sum of the coefficients from the original method. For example, in the case of no controls, the coefficient on the calculus class dummy variable was 0.51. If we assume that students who

Table C.3

Log Earnings OLS Regressions

	(1)	(2)	(3)	(4)	(5)
Vocational math	0.001	−0.011	−0.024**	−0.027**	−0.029**
	(0.011)	(0.010)	(0.011)	(0.010)	(0.010)
Pre-algebra	0.067**	0.042**	0.023*	0.007	0.006
	(0.014)	(0.014)	(0.014)	(0.014)	(0.014)
Algebra/geometry	0.080**	0.061**	0.061**	0.031**	0.027**
	(0.010)	(0.010)	(0.010)	(0.010)	(0.010)
Intermediate algebra	0.109**	0.086**	0.078**	0.032**	0.021
	(0.017)	(0.016)	(0.016)	(0.016)	(0.016)
Advanced algebra	0.134**	0.100**	0.088**	0.042**	0.034**
	(0.014)	(0.014)	(0.014)	(0.014)	(0.014)
Calculus	0.195**	0.151**	0.120**	0.065**	0.057*
	(0.033)	(0.032)	(0.032)	(0.032)	(0.032)
Ethnicity = Hispanic		0.027	0.036*	0.042**	0.047**
		(0.019)	(0.021)	(0.021)	(0.021)
Ethnicity = black		−0.006	−0.0002	−0.009	−0.014
		(0.024)	(0.0249)	(0.025)	(0.024)
Ethnicity = Asian		0.041	0.023	−0.006	−0.010
		(0.042)	(0.043)	(0.042)	(0.042)
Ethnicity = Native American		−0.109**	−0.068	−0.059	−0.061
		(0.051)	(0.051)	(0.050)	(0.050)
Ethnicity = other		0.004	0.002	−0.030	−0.043
		(0.108)	(0.107)	(0.106)	(0.105)
Male		0.267**	0.272**	0.292**	0.293**
		(0.014)	(0.014)	(0.014)	(0.014)
Age as of 6/15/91		−0.055**	−0.042**	−0.023*	−0.024*
		(0.013)	(0.013)	(0.013)	(0.013)
Number of siblings		−0.013**	−0.009**	−0.006	−0.006
		(0.004)	(0.004)	(0.004)	(0.004)
Married in 1991		0.025*	0.038**	0.049**	0.046**
		(0.014)	(0.014)	(0.014)	(0.014)
Family income: <$7K		−0.151**	−0.124**	−0.106**	−0.109**
		(0.032)	(0.032)	(0.031)	(0.031)
Family income: $7K–$15K		−0.037*	−0.025	−0.021	−0.019
		(0.022)	(0.022)	(0.021)	(0.021)
Family income: $15K–$20K		−0.005	0.001	0.003	0.007
		(0.024)	(0.023)	(0.023)	(0.023)

Table C.3 (continued)

	(1)	(2)	(3)	(4)	(5)
Family income: $25K–$38K		0.074**	0.070**	0.064**	0.066**
		(0.025)	(0.025)	(0.024)	(0.024)
Family income: $38K and up		0.068**	0.059**	0.052*	0.057**
		(0.029)	(0.029)	(0.028)	(0.028)
Family income: missing		0.011	0.004	0.038	0.037
		(0.036)	(0.036)	(0.036)	(0.035)
At least one parent U.S. native		–0.079**	–0.026	–0.009	–0.004
		(0.026)	(0.026)	(0.026)	(0.026)
Education mother: < high school graduate		–0.071**	–0.062**	–0.055**	–0.054*
		(0.022)	(0.022)	(0.022)	(0.022)
Education mother: vocational		–0.030	–0.031	–0.040	–0.035
		(0.029)	(0.029)	(0.029)	(0.029)
Education mother: some college		0.015	0.015	–0.005	0.002
		(0.026)	(0.026)	(0.026)	(0.026)
Education mother: college graduate		0.000	–0.004	–0.035	–0.032
		(0.032)	(0.032)	(0.031)	(0.031)
Education mother: master's degree, Ph.D.		–0.051	–0.050	–0.075*	–0.065
		(0.043)	(0.042)	(0.042)	(0.041)
Education mother: missing		–0.026	–0.028	–0.024	–0.024
		(0.023)	(0.023)	(0.022)	(0.022)
Education father: < high school graduate		–0.050**	–0.044*	–0.038*	–0.038*
		(0.023)	(0.023)	(0.023)	(0.023)
Education father: vocational		0.000	–0.001	–0.008	–0.005
		(0.031)	(0.031)	(0.030)	(0.030)
Education father: some college		0.026	0.024	0.007	0.009
		(0.029)	(0.029)	(0.028)	(0.028)
Education father: college graduate		0.051	0.039	0.005	0.001
		(0.031)	(0.031)	(0.031)	(0.031)
Education father: master's degree, Ph.D.		0.064*	0.057*	0.015	0.018
		(0.035)	(0.034)	(0.034)	(0.034)
Education father: missing		–0.017	–0.023	–0.024	–0.021
		(0.022)	(0.022)	(0.022)	(0.021)
Teachers unionized			0.024	0.020	0.019
			(0.023)	(0.023)	(0.022)
Union status missing			0.038	0.018	0.008
			(0.073)	(0.072)	(0.072)

Table C.3 (continued)

	(1)	(2)	(3)	(4)	(5)
Alternative high school			0.035	0.034	0.030
			(0.048)	(0.047)	(0.047)
Cuban Hispanic public school			0.149**	0.146**	0.143**
			(0.065)	(0.064)	(0.064)
Other Hispanic public school			0.042	0.034	0.032
			(0.029)	(0.028)	(0.028)
Student teacher ratio			0.0003	0.0005	0.0008
			(0.0022)	(0.0022)	(0.0022)
Books per pupil			−0.0002	−0.0001	0.0001
			(0.0008)	(0.0008)	(0.0008)
High school membership (1,000s)			0.020	0.016	0.014
			(0.010)	(0.010)	(0.010)
Days in school year			0.003	0.003	0.002
			(0.003)	(0.003)	(0.003)
Proportion disadvantaged students			−0.105**	−0.074**	−0.076*
			(0.042)	(0.041)	(0.041)
Proportion of teachers with master's degree			0.011	0.012	0.010
			(0.034)	(0.034)	(0.034)
District average spending per pupil ($1,000s)			0.013	0.011	0.014
			(0.010)	(0.010)	(0.010)
Teacher's salary ($1,000)			−0.003	−0.001	0.001
			(0.010)	(0.010)	(0.010)
Suburban			0.013	0.012	0.012
			(0.020)	(0.020)	(0.019)
Rural			−0.043*	−0.051**	−0.051**
			(0.023)	(0.023)	(0.023)
New England			0.082**	0.078*	0.082**
			(0.042)	(0.041)	(0.041)
Middle Atlantic			0.025	0.007	0.008
			(0.034)	(0.033)	(0.033)
South Atlantic			−0.035	−0.031	−0.031
			(0.031)	(0.031)	(0.030)
East South Central			−0.057	−0.059	−0.069*
			(0.038)	(0.038)	(0.038)
West South Central			−0.121**	−0.125**	−0.127**
			(0.033)	(0.033)	(0.032)

Table C.3 (continued)

	(1)	(2)	(3)	(4)	(5)
East North Central			−0.048	−0.059**	−0.062**
			(0.029)	(0.029)	(0.029)
West North Central			−0.077**	−0.093**	−0.096**
			(0.036)	(0.035)	(0.035)
Mountain			−0.150**	−0.153**	−0.151**
			(0.038)	(0.037)	(0.037)
Native value missing		−0.086**	−0.058	−0.049	−0.042
		(0.035)	(0.035)	(0.035)	(0.035)
Number of siblings missing		−0.140**	−0.115*	−0.097	−0.088
		(0.069)	(0.069)	(0.068)	(0.068)
Marital status missing		−0.078	−0.083	−0.059	−0.059
		(0.095)	(0.094)	(0.093)	(0.092)
Student/teacher ratio missing			0.002	−0.011	0.000
			(0.062)	(0.061)	(0.061)
Books per pupil missing			−0.008	0.005	0.007
			(0.036)	(0.036)	(0.036)
High school membership missing			0.003	0.008	0.003
			(0.059)	(0.058)	(0.058)
Days in school year missing			0.609	0.523	0.477
			(0.494)	(0.486)	(0.483)
% disadvantaged students missing			−0.007	−0.008	−0.009
			(0.027)	(0.027)	(0.027)
% teachers with master's degree missing			0.078	0.068	0.061
			(0.050)	(0.049)	(0.049)
District spending missing			0.040	0.038	0.045
			(0.028)	(0.028)	(0.028)
Teacher's salary missing			−0.066	−0.043	−0.024
			(0.081)	(0.080)	(0.079)
Higher than bachelor's degree				0.342**	0.358**
				(0.044)	(0.047)
Bachelor's degree				0.256**	0.253**
				(0.023)	(0.028)
Associate's degree				0.181**	0.157**
				(0.027)	(0.030)
Certificate				0.048*	0.045*
				(0.025)	(0.025)

Table C.3 (continued)

	(1)	(2)	(3)	(4)	(5)
Some postsecondary education but no degree				0.054** (0.020)	0.056** (0.021)
Less than high school				−0.140** (0.034)	−0.142** (0.033)
Degree missing				−0.018 (0.075)	−0.021 (0.074)
Business major					0.181** (0.037)
Engineering major					0.269** (0.042)
Health major					0.372** (0.047)
Other major					0.027 (0.058)
Science major					0.065 (0.054)
Social science major					0.096** (0.042)
Technical major					0.033 (0.058)
Intercept	9.700** (0.020)	11.225** (0.349)	10.269** (0.607)	9.759** (0.599)	9.676** (0.596)
R-squared	0.069	0.151	0.172	0.199	0.212
No. of observations	5,919	5,919	5,919	5,919	5,919

NOTES: Standard errors are in parentheses. The percentage change in earnings is given by $(e^\beta - 1) * 100\%$, where β is the regression coefficient. Column 1 includes only math curriculum measures. Column 2 adds controls for demographic and family characteristics. Columns 3, 4, and 5 add controls for school characteristics, highest degree attained, and postsecondary education major, respectively. All models contain an intercept. We do not weight the regressions because we include the variables upon which the sample was stratified for the models in columns 3, 4, and 5. We also estimate the model in column 4 but include only the courses that the student passed in the count of math courses. The coefficients barely change. See the section on GPA in Appendix A for details on how we compute the number of courses completed. Note that in this table we report the effect of the proportion of disadvantaged students and teachers with a master's degree, whereas in Table C.1 we report the mean percentage values of these variables.

**Significant at the 5 percent level; *significant at the 10 percent level.

completed calculus also completed one course each of algebra, intermediate algebra, and advanced algebra, the original coefficient values indicated that such a student would have earnings approximately 51 percent higher than would somebody who did not. This exactly equals the sum of algebra/geometry, intermediate algebra, advanced algebra, and calculus (the typical course sequence of students who end up with calculus as their highest class) coefficients on the math credit measures in our original model (column 1 of Table C.3). The corresponding sums of math credit coefficients and dummy variable coefficients are close in all model specifications, but there are some differences. This is because in a minority of cases, math credits within each level did not equal zero or one. Some students earned only half a credit in a category; sometimes they earned two. Nonetheless, the similar results from these two methods of measurement assures us that our original curriculum measures are robust to this change in specification.

Explanation of Ability Bias

Assume that the true earnings data generating process is:

$$\ln w_{is} = \alpha + \lambda Curric_{is} + \beta_1 Demo_{is} + \beta_2 Fam_{is} + \\ \beta_3 Sch_{is} + \beta_4 HiDeg_{is} + \beta_5 Abil_{is} + \upsilon_{is} \tag{2}$$

where $Abil_{is}$ is the student's innate ability, β_5 is the effect of a one-unit change in ability on log-earnings, and υ_{is} is an i.i.d. error term. If we estimate the original model (1) instead of this true one, then ability appears in the error term in the form of $\varepsilon_{is} = \beta_5 Abil_{is} + \upsilon_{is}$. To see how the potential bias arises, consider the special case in which earnings are modeled as a function of a constant and a single measure of curriculum (such as the total number of math credits earned). In this case, the estimated coefficient on curriculum measure k has the expectation:

$$E(\hat{\lambda}_k) = \lambda_k + \beta_5 \frac{\sigma_{Curric_k, Ability}}{\sigma^2_{Curric_k}}$$

where $\sigma_{x,y}$ is the covariance between x and y and σ^2_x is the variance of x. Thus, the estimated curriculum coefficient is biased if there is any correlation between ability and the curriculum measure.[6] This same principle holds in the multivariate case, except that the degree of bias is composed of the correlation between ability and all the other explanatory factors.

Instrumental Variables Results

As described in Chapter 5, one way we attempt to curb potential omitted ability/motivation bias is by adding controls for math GPA, math test score, and student and parent attitudes to our original model (see Table C.4 for detailed regression results). In another attempt to mitigate this bias, we follow Altonji's lead and use a school's average math credits earned in each of the six math categories as instruments for the student's own math credits earned in those categories. The intuition behind this approach is as follows. We want to purge the portion of the curriculum effect that is really caused by ability or motivation. We use the *school's average curriculum* (the instrument), as well as the other student background information from the original model, to predict the student's actual curriculum. Any portion of the student's actual curriculum above or below the predicted level is assumed to be caused by variations in ability (or motivation) from the average ability or motivation in the school, thus leaving the predicted value independent of ability. In other words, students of the same background, attending schools with equivalent curriculum patterns, should be taking the same curriculum. Any difference between the curriculum the student takes and the average curriculum taken by other students at that school, after accounting for personal traits, is assumed to be caused by variations in ability and motivation within the school. Therefore, if we use this predicted level of curriculum in our model in lieu of the actual level, we will be estimating the effect of pure curriculum rather than the effect of a mix of curriculum, ability, and motivation. Because we are using the school's average math credits earned in each of the six math categories as predictors of the student's own math credits earned in those categories,

---

[6]Bias occurs when the expected value of the estimated coefficient is not equal to the true value of the coefficient.

Table C.4

Log Earnings Models: OLS Regression Results with Various Ability and Motivation Controls

	(1)	(2)	(3)	(4)	(5)	(6)
Vocational math	−0.027**	−0.029**	−0.023**	−0.027**	−0.028**	−0.033**
	(0.010)	(0.011)	(0.012)	(0.011)	(0.012)	(0.012)
Pre-algebra	0.007	0.005	0.006	0.002	0.005	−0.002
	(0.014)	(0.014)	(0.015)	(0.015)	(0.015)	(0.015)
Algebra/geometry	0.031**	0.029**	0.025**	0.032**	0.026**	0.024**
	(0.010)	(0.010)	(0.011)	(0.011)	(0.011)	(0.011)
Intermediate algebra	0.032**	0.022	0.018	0.024	0.012	0.012
	(0.016)	(0.017)	(0.018)	(0.017)	(0.018)	(0.018)
Advanced algebra	0.042**	0.029**	0.027*	0.035**	0.019	0.013
	(0.014)	(0.015)	(0.016)	(0.015)	(0.016)	(0.016)
Calculus	0.065**	0.047	0.055*	0.065 **	0.045	0.045
	(0.032)	(0.032)	(0.034)	(0.032)	(0.034)	(0.034)
Math GPA		0.036 **			0.034 **	0.037**
		(0.009)			(0.010)	(0.010)
Math test score			0.003 **		0.002	0.001
			(0.001)		(0.001)	(0.001)
Attitudes				Yes		Yes
R-squared	0.199	0.201	0.199	0.208	0.200	0.208
No. of observations	5,919	5,896	5,138	5,344	5,119	4,944

NOTES: Standard errors are in parentheses. All models include an intercept as well as controls for the demographic, family, school, and highest-degree variables that we presented in Table 5.1. The models do not control for college major, because we want that effect to be attributed to curriculum for reasons cited in the text. Adding dummy variables for college major changes the coefficients only minimally. The coefficients in column 5 become: −0.029, 0.003, 0.022, 0.004, 0.013, and 0.041. We also estimate the models in column 1 and 2 but include only the courses that the student passed in the count of math courses. The coefficients barely change. See the section on GPA in Appendix A for details on how we compute the number of courses completed.

** Significant at the 5 percent level; *significant at the 10 percent level.

the school's average curriculum measures are considered the instrumental variables.[7]

A valid instrument must be correlated with the student's curriculum but not correlated with the error term. Judging by actual estimates, the school's average curriculum within each category is highly correlated with the student's own level. It will not be correlated with the error term if the distribution of students within each school is the same. However, if some schools are higher-ability schools because, for example, parents of highly motivated students all flock to the same school, then the instrument will not fully eliminate bias resulting from unobserved variation in student ability or motivation. Nonetheless, for the reasons provided in Chapter 5, and given the dearth of other instrument candidates, we are confident that these IV estimates enable some useful inference.

The results from using instrumental variables to estimate the model are presented in Table C.5. In the first stage of this two-stage least squares procedure, we regress each of the six math curriculum measures on each of the six school average curriculum variables and the full set of independent variables. In the second stage, we substitute the predicted curriculum values for the actual curriculum values and estimate the log-earnings models as before. We limit the regression to observations for which there are more than four other students from the same school. We do this to calculate meaningful average curriculum values.[8]

---

[7]Altonji (1995) introduced the idea of using the school's average curriculum as an instrument for the student's curriculum.

[8]We exclude the student's own curriculum when calculating the school average curriculum for that student. In our second-stage regression, we exclude students who come from schools where the school average curriculum was calculated using fewer than four observations. This requirement causes us to exclude about 4 percent of the students. The results change only minimally if we change the requirement for the number of observations for computing the average from each school. The number of students per school ranges from 1 to 36, with a median of about 12. We try an alternative specification where we estimate the first-stage regressions using the largest possible sample of students, including those students whom we exclude from the second-stage regression because they have missing earnings data. Although this may help to increase the school information and might include students who are less able and not in our earnings sample because they are not employed, the results change only minimally.

Table C.5

Log Earnings Models: OLS, Instrumental Variables Estimation, and School Fixed-Effects Results With and Without Ability and Motivation Controls

	(1)	(2)	(3)	(4)	(5)	(6)
Vocational math	−0.027**	−0.029**	−0.084**	−0.086**	−0.019	−0.023*
	(0.010)	(0.011)	(0.030)	(0.030)	(0.012)	(0.013)
Pre-algebra	0.007	0.005	0.015	0.013	0.006	0.004
	(0.014)	(0.014)	(0.034)	(0.034)	(0.017)	(0.017)
Algebra/geometry	0.031**	0.029**	0.090**	0.083**	0.029**	0.027**
	(0.010)	(0.010)	(0.035)	(0.035)	(0.012)	(0.012)
Intermediate algebra	0.032**	0.022	−0.107	−0.100	0.054**	0.042**
	(0.016)	(0.017)	(0.068)	(0.067)	(0.019)	(0.019)
Advanced algebra	0.042**	0.029**	−0.077	−0.082	0.054**	0.039**
	(0.014)	(0.015)	(0.050)	(0.050)	(0.017)	(0.017)
Calculus	0.065**	0.047	−0.132	−0.140	0.077**	0.058
	(0.032)	(0.032)	(0.167)	(0.167)	(0.036)	(0.036)
Math GPA		0.036**		0.063**		0.039**
		(0.009)		(0.015)		(0.009)
Estimation method	OLS	OLS	IV	IV	FE	FE
R-squared	0.199	0.201	0.187	0.192	0.316	0.319
No. of observations	5,919	5,896	5,864	5,841	5,919	5,896

NOTES: Standard errors are in parentheses. All models include an intercept as well as controls for the demographic, family, school, and highest-degree variables that we presented in Table 5.1. The models do not control for college major, because we want that effect to be attributed to curriculum for reasons cited in the text. Columns 1 and 2 repeat the OLS estimates from columns 1 and 2 of Table C.4 for easy comparison with the OLS model that controls for GPA. Columns 3 and 4 contain the IV results. Columns 5 and 6 contain the OLS with high school fixed-effects results. For the first-stage regressions in each IV-estimated model, the p-values for the F-test of the hypothesis that the coefficients on the six school-average instruments are equal to zero are 0.0001.

**Significant at the 5 percent level; *significant at the 10 percent level.

The first two columns repeat the results from the linear regressions, and we use these as baseline comparisons. The model in column 1 does not control for GPA, whereas the model in column 2 does. Column 3 shows the IV results with no additional ability controls, whereas column

4 adds GPA controls.[9] The results are strikingly similar across both IV specifications. Vocational math is significant and negative in both cases. More interesting, though, credits earned in the algebra/geometry category are significant at the 5 percent level in both specifications and are of similar magnitude at approximately 8 to 9 percent. This is a rather large increase from the baseline comparison case. It appears that the effect of higher-level math courses has been condensed into the algebra/geometry category. It is important to stress that although the higher-level math coefficients now have negative signs, they are measured so imprecisely that they are not significantly different from zero.[10] We conclude that although these IV estimates differ from the other models in specifics, they continue to suggest that math curriculum has important predicted effects on earnings about a decade after high school.

As another robustness check, we use OLS to estimate a model with high school fixed effects. Whereas the IV estimates should net out ability effects within each school, the fixed-effects estimates should control for across-school variations in ability. These results appear in the last two columns of Table C.5. When we do this without GPA in the model, the coefficients on the curriculum variables rise by about .01 relative to the comparable OLS estimate model without fixed effects, except for pre-algebra and algebra/geometry coefficients, where they are unchanged. Further, the coefficient on vocational math is no longer significant.

Additional High School Subjects

This section of the appendix contains the OLS and IV regression output for the models that include measures of math, English, science, and foreign language curriculum (see Table C.6). For each estimation method (OLS and IV), we present a comparison model that includes only math in the curriculum measure. Once again, when we use the IV technique, the school's average curriculum in each category of each

---

[9]We do not control for math IRT test score because we are concerned that it overcontrols for ability.

[10]Given that few students take the high-level math courses, the quality of the instrument may be reduced for this level of course, therefore explaining the lack of precision in estimating these coefficients.

Table C.6

Log Earnings Models (OLS and IV) with Specific Math, English, Science, and Foreign Language Courses

	OLS		IV	
	(1)	(2)	(3)	(4)
Vocational math	−0.027**	−0.030**	−0.084**	−0.075*
	(0.010)	(0.011)	(0.030)	(0.039)
Pre-algebra	0.007	0.004	0.015	0.030
	(0.014)	(0.014)	(0.034)	(0.045)
Algebra/geometry	0.031**	0.020*	0.090**	0.097**
	(0.010)	(0.011)	(0.035)	(0.044)
Intermediate algebra	0.032**	0.019	−0.107	−0.129
	(0.016)	(0.017)	(0.068)	(0.082)
Advanced algebra	0.042**	0.030**	−0.077	−0.093
	(0.014)	(0.015)	(0.050)	(0.058)
Calculus	0.065**	0.043	−0.132	−0.162
	(0.032)	(0.033)	(0.167)	(0.171)
Below-level English		0.004		0.019
		(0.013)		(0.033)
Average English		0.015**		0.025
		(0.008)		(0.024)
English literature courses		0.015*		0.034
		(0.009)		(0.029)
Above-level English		0.026**		0.071**
		(0.013)		(0.036)
Basic biology		−0.008		−0.080*
		(0.019)		(0.046)
General biology		−0.015		−0.069*
		(0.013)		(0.040)
Primary physics		−0.023**		−0.060*
		(0.012)		(0.031)
Secondary physics		0.005		0.143
		(0.034)		(0.100)
Chemistry 1, physics 1		0.020		−0.004
		(0.014)		(0.060)
Chemistry 2, physics 2, advanced placement biology		0.020		0.028
		(0.020)		(0.073)
Foreign language (1–2 credits)		0.025		−0.024
		(0.017)		(0.104)

Table C.6 (continued)

	OLS		IV	
	(1)	(2)	(3)	(4)
Foreign language (3–4 credits)		0.054**		0.129
		(0.026)		(0.143)
R-squared	0.199	0.200	0.187	0.186
No. of observations	5,919	5,735	5,864	5,681

NOTES: Standard errors are in parentheses. All models control for demographic, family, school, and educational attainment characteristics. See Table 5.1 for a complete list. Each model contains an intercept. Column 1 repeats the model from column 4 of Table C.3 for easier comparison. Column 3 repeats the model from column 3 of Table C.5 for easier comparison. For the first-stage regressions in each IV model, the p-values for the F-test of the hypothesis that the coefficients on the instruments are equal to zero are 0.0001.

**Significant at the 5 percent level; *significant at the 10 percent level.

subject provides the instruments for the student's actual curriculum. We omit math GPA from these models and rely primarily on the instrumental variables estimator to eliminate the ability/motivation portion of the curriculum effects.

The estimated math effects once we control for additional curriculum measures are remarkably similar to the IV results from the model with math as the only curriculum variable (compare column 4 to column 3).

Our results indicate that the mathematics curriculum has a very large effect on earnings, regardless of whether we also control for other types of courses taken. In fact, the IV estimates imply that the returns to taking a one-unit algebra/geometry course are statistically significant and large in magnitude—about 9 percent. This is higher than the returns to an additional year of schooling (often cited as 7 percent).

In contrast to the OLS estimated model that contains all four curriculum measures, the effect of the above-average English credits in the IV estimated model is more than doubled, but that of its counterpart, foreign language, is no longer statistically significant. Perhaps accumulating credits in foreign language is a sign of ability or motivation, which the IV method eliminates. Finally, in the IV estimated model, the low-level science courses are still predicted to have negative, and now even larger, statistically significant effects.

Comparison to Previous Research

A vast amount of literature is devoted to distinguishing the human capital effects from the signaling effects of schooling, yet the debate is far from resolved. However, it is worthwhile at this point to discuss the evidence to date regarding curriculum's effect on earnings. The economics literature has been slow to incorporate high school curriculum in the standard education production function, but two recent studies have addressed the issue: Altonji (1995) and Levine and Zimmerman (1995).[11]

Altonji (1995)

Altonji attempts to ascertain the value of an additional year of high school courses in hopes of answering the question: Does an extra year of education serve merely as a screening device or do the courses that make up that year possess some intrinsic value as well? He uses the National Longitudinal Survey of the High School Class of 1972 (NLS72). In particular, he uses the number of credits that students complete in eight different subjects during grades 10, 11, and 12, as well as rich data about family background and high school characteristics.[12] He models the log-wage of each person as a linear function of the credits that the student completes, standard background characteristics, and years of postsecondary education. Because the eight curriculum variables are highly correlated with one another,[13] he conducts the same analysis using

---

[11]Gamoran (1998) provides an excellent review of other studies that have undertaken similar goals. Most of these studies are quite dated and are not in the economics literature. Many focus on the effects of tracking rather than specific high school courses. Others that do look at courses restrict their samples to students who obtain no postsecondary education.

[12]The eight subjects are science, math, English, social studies, foreign language, industrial arts, commercial courses, and fine arts.

[13]This means that an overestimate of one course's coefficient could coincide with an underestimate of the coefficient on a different course.

combinations of courses by subject instead of entering the individual courses separately.

He uses three methods to estimate the effects of the curriculum: basic OLS models, OLS models with high school fixed effects, and an instrumental variables approach in which he uses a school's average number of credits earned per student within each subject as an instrument for each student's number of credits earned.[14] All three approaches lead to similar results. Altonji's overall conclusion is that "the effect of a year equivalent of courses is much smaller than the value of one year in high school." In other words, the whole is greater than the sum of its parts. Even before controlling for background characteristics and using the IV approach, each additional year of science, math, English, social studies, and foreign language combined leads to a minuscule 0.3 percent increase in wages. He finds stronger curriculum effects if he excludes the (negative) effects of English and social studies. An additional year of math, science, and foreign language increases earnings by 3.3 percent.[15] Because an additional year of school is estimated to increase wages by 7 percent, Altonji's results lend support to the view that high school serves as a screening device rather than as a mechanism for human capital formation.

Levine and Zimmerman (1995)

Levine and Zimmerman, citing the important role of highly skilled service-sector jobs in the economy, conduct research that focuses on the effect that math and science courses have on wages. They use data from two main sources: the National Longitudinal Survey of Youth (NLSY) and HSB's 1980 senior cohort. Whereas Altonji studied a group of students who graduated in 1972, Levine and Zimmerman focus on students who graduated in the late 1970s through the early 1980s in the case of the NLSY and students who graduated in 1980 in the case of the

---

[14]We discuss how this removes the individual variation that could be correlated with ability or motivation earlier in this appendix.

[15]OLS estimates are slightly larger, and OLS with high school fixed effects are substantially larger. If he looks at the isolated effect of mathematics, he finds that an additional year of math leads to an earnings increase of 1.8 percent, but that disappears once he controls for ability.

HSB survey. Like Altonji, they use the number of credits earned in math and science courses (separately) as their curriculum measures in the HSB data. Another noteworthy aspect of their work is that they are the first to estimate separate models for men and women.

Levine and Zimmerman find that science classes have very little effect on wages for either males or females. They find that math credits have an effect on females' wages, but not on males' wages.[16] However, this effect is limited to women who have completed some college or have earned a college degree. For female college graduates, an additional semester of math during high school is predicted to lead to a 5.4 percent increase in log wages.[17] One factor that may be confounding their results is that the authors do not distinguish between public and private schools. If private schools are more academically inclined, the measured curriculum effect may really be picking up a private school effect.

Contributions of This Report

A key factor that distinguishes our study from the two earlier contributions to the literature is our detailed analysis of the *types* of math courses that students take. A second distinguishing factor is our focus on the role, if any, that high school curriculum plays in creating the well-known wage gaps between workers of different races and ethnicities.

Like Levine and Zimmerman, we use the HSB dataset, which in our view is the most recent nationally representative dataset that follows students into the workforce, while providing detailed curriculum information. Unlike Levine and Zimmerman, we use the sophomore cohort of the HSB dataset, most of whose members graduated from high school in 1982, rather than the senior cohort that graduated in 1980. This alternative sample provides several advantages. First, the Levine and Zimmerman wage data reflect earnings six years after graduation rather than 10, as in our case. It seems possible that the effects of curriculum

---

[16]In their models using the HSB data, Levine and Zimmerman find that math courses do have an effect for men with a high school diploma or some postsecondary education. This result does not carry over to the NLSY data.

[17]It disappears when they use Altonji's IV technique.

on earnings could look quite different for workers in their late twenties than for a sample of 24-year-olds who, to some extent, have not yet settled into careers. Second, the transcript data for the 1982 HSB seniors is much more detailed than for the 1980 HSB seniors. Third, both Levine and Zimmerman and Altonji study a cohort of seniors, thus excluding high school dropouts. Because we begin with a grade 10 cohort, we are able to include some dropouts in our models. Fourth, we use a completely separate HSB sample from the one used by Levine and Zimmerman, allowing for a largely independent test of the effects of curriculum. Fifth, whereas Altonji examines earnings in the 1970s and in 1986, and Levine and Zimmerman examine earnings in 1986, we follow the students into the early 1990s. Given the dramatic increase in the returns to education in the United States between the late 1970s and the mid 1990s, it seems important to estimate the relation between curriculum and earnings using a recent set of wage observations.

To highlight the difference that classifying courses by their type makes, we re-estimated our earnings models using the aggregate credits earned in a particular subject rather than the detailed credit counts.[18] We then compare the results from our aggregate model to Altonji's (1995) results. We present the outcomes from the aggregate model in Table C.7 (for models estimated with OLS and IV). Once again, all models control for demographic, family, school, and educational attainment characteristics. Because we are no longer using the academic level of curriculum, we also include a control for the student's self-reported high school track (academic, general, vocational, etc.). This leaves a model that is very similar to Altonji's.

Estimating with OLS yields a predicted effect from the aggregated math measure that is an average of the effects when the math curriculum levels are entered separately.[19] However, when we include all four subject areas in the model, the aggregate math effect drops by almost 50

---

[18]Rather than relying on the pre-calculated course counts provided in HSB, we calculate the total number of credits earned directly from the transcript data.

[19]This can be seen by comparing the average of the math effects from models 1 and 2 of Table C.6 to the math effects in models 1 and 2 of Table C.7.

Table C.7

Log Earnings Models (OLS and IV) with Aggregate Math, English, and Foreign Language Courses

	OLS		IV	
	(1)	(2)	(3)	(4)
Math	0.024**	0.014*	−0.010	−0.027
	(0.007)	(0.008)	(0.024)	(0.033)
English		0.012		0.028
		(0.007)		(0.022)
Science		0.005		−0.025
		(0.008)		(0.026)
Foreign language		0.023**		0.028
		(0.007)		(0.031)
R-squared	0.192	0.193	0.191	0.190
No. of observations	5,919	5,735	5,864	5,681

NOTES: Standard errors are in parentheses. All models control for demographic, family, school, and educational attainment characteristics. See Table 5.1 for a complete list. These regressions also control for the track (academic, general, or vocational) in which the student participated. For the first-stage regressions in each IV model, the p-values for the F-test of the hypothesis that the coefficients on the instruments are equal to zero are 0.0001. Excluding high school dropouts from the analysis changes the results only minimally (on the order of 0.002).

**Significant at the 5 percent level; *significant at the 10 percent level.

percent and is no longer statistically significant at the 5 percent level.[20] A similar pattern is evident with English curriculum. Whereas aggregate English credits do not appear to affect earnings, when they enter the model separately based on their academic level, they do matter and the effects vary by the level of the class.[21] The foreign language effect is still significant in the aggregate model and larger than in the disaggregated

---

[20]This can been by comparing the math effects between models 1 and 2 of Table C.7.

[21]This can be seen by comparing the English effects in model 2 of Table C.6 to the aggregate English effect in model 2 of Table C.7.

case, indicating that it may be picking up the effects of some of the other subjects. When we estimate these aggregate models using instrumental variables, none of the curriculum effects are statistically significant at the 5 percent level.

What is encouraging to note is that the results from the models with aggregate course counts in the four subjects are extremely similar to the results from comparable models in Altonji (1995).[22] This gives us confidence that our method of classifying the curriculum by level may be helping to explain some of the "curriculum puzzle."[23] To further approximate Altonji's results, we estimated these models but excluded students who did not graduate from high school. The results changed minimally, with the predicted effects differing by 0.002 at the most. We had originally hypothesized that our results might differ from Altonji's because we are using a more recent cohort and have included high school dropouts in our analysis. Now it seems clear that the differences stem mostly from our more detailed classification of curriculum.

As we point out in the main text, this finding has many implications for curriculum reform. Merely increasing the number of courses required of students may not achieve the desired effect. It will be important to focus on the type of courses students are required to take as well.

---

[22]This applies to models estimated by both OLS and IV methods.

[23]This term was coined by Altonji when describing the small estimated effects of curriculum.

Appendix D

Testing for Variations in the Effectiveness of Math Among Subgroups of Students

The California Model

Because we cannot precisely estimate a separate model for California, we perform two procedures to determine how the national models might compare to a California model. We first add a series of California interaction terms to the national model and show more specifically that the math effects are not different if the student is from California.[1] We also show that the relationship between math courses and other explanatory factors in the model is the same for students both in California high schools and in high schools in the rest of the nation. This ensemble of results gives us confidence that the national model does indeed apply to California. When we conduct this further analysis, we concentrate on the baseline earnings model that controls for demographic, parental, and high school characteristics, as well as the highest educational degree attained by the student. However, the results hold if we also control for ability and motivation in the form of math GPA. Below we describe these examinations in more detail. To conserve space, we do not include related regression output.

Are Math Effects California-Dependent?

We find that curriculum effects do not depend on whether the student attends a California high school. Our strategy is to add six

---

[1] We would like to thank Steve Rivkin for the algorithm that identifies the California schools in HSB.

variables to the national model that interact the math curriculum variables with a variable that describes whether the student is from California.[2] The math effects in this model are comparable to those in the corresponding national model. Because none of the California interaction terms are statistically significant, this indicates that the curriculum effects for students do not depend on whether the student attends a California high school. Of course, the size of our California sample may be limiting our ability to discern minor differences in the effect of curriculum.

Relationship Between Math Credits and Other Explanatory Factors

As an additional check to ensure that a California model would yield similar results to the national model, we determine that the relationship between the math curriculum variables and the remaining explanatory variables is the same in the California sample as it is in the rest of the nation. To do this, we estimate a model of math credits as a function of demographic, parental, and school characteristics.[3] But to this regression, we add a series of interaction terms where a California dummy variable is interacted with each of the explanatory variables. If the interaction terms are significant, we can say that the relationship between the explanatory variables is different in California and therefore the state-specific model may actually lead to somewhat different curriculum effects. However, when we do this, generally we find that the relationship is the same within and outside of the California sample.[4]

---

[2]We also include the dummy variable indicating California status to allow for a noncurriculum state effect.

[3]This is the same strategy that we used to determine whether the relationship between the explanatory factors of the model was the same for observations in and out of the regression sample.

[4]Because there are six different measures of math credits, we regress each of the measures on the interaction terms and remaining explanatory variables, which leaves us with six models to decipher. Because there are so many explanatory factors, there are equally as many interaction terms. If the same interaction term was significant in three of the six models, we consider it to potentially indicate a difference between California and national schools. We flagged the four variables that satisfied this criterion and interacted them with the California dummy variable in a regular earnings model to ensure that such

Math Effects and Gender

As we discussed in Chapter 6, there may be differences in the way math affects earnings for men and for women. Table D.1 shows the regression coefficients and standard errors that correspond to the results presented in Table 6.1. The main text provides an analysis of this table.

Do Math Effects Depend on Certain School or Student Characteristics?

As we pointed out in Chapter 6, we do not have large enough samples from any particular population of interest to estimate separate models. Although we do control for a variety of student and school characteristics, we probe the question of whether certain of these characteristics make math more effective by adding a series of terms to our baseline model to interact school characteristics with math credits.[5] For example, to determine the extent to which math effects depend on the percentage of teachers at the student's school with a master's degree, we add six new explanatory variables to our model. These variables are the student's math credits earned in each of the six math courses multiplied by the percentage of teachers with a master's degree at the student's school. The math effects in this new model are composed of a pure math effect *plus* an additional effect that is a function of that particular school input measure. Another interpretation is that the effect of these interaction variables represents the *additional* effect that each math course is predicted to have, given a change of one percentage point in the percentage of teachers with a master's degree.

In a series of models, we include interaction terms separately for each of the school quality measures in which we are interested. In other

---

model specification does not alter the results. It does not. The math curriculum coefficients barely change.

[5]The baseline model is the one in which the log of 1991 earnings is specified to be a function of math curriculum, student demographic traits, the student's family and school characteristics, the student's math GPA, and the student's highest educational degree attained. For the most part, the results in this appendix also hold if we do not control for GPA or highest degree.

Table D.1

The Effect of an Additional Math Credit on the Log of 1991 Earnings, by Gender

	Male		Female	
	(1)	(2)	(3)	(4)
Vocational math	–0.024*	–0.026**	–0.040**	–0.040**
	(0.013)	(0.013)	(0.018)	(0.018)
Pre-algebra	0.009	0.001	0.022	0.005
	(0.018)	(0.017)	(0.022)	(0.022)
Algebra/geometry	0.036**	0.012	0.072**	0.045**
	(0.013)	(0.013)	(0.016)	(0.016)
Intermediate algebra	0.057**	0.024	0.050**	0.014
	(0.021)	(0.022)	(0.025)	(0.025)
Advanced algebra	0.048**	0.015	0.082**	0.049**
	(0.019)	(0.019)	(0.022)	(0.022)
Calculus	0.041	0.009	0.134**	0.090**
	(0.042)	(0.042)	(0.049)	(0.049)
Math GPA	0.060**	0.040**	0.053**	0.035**
	(0.011)	(0.011)	(0.013)	(0.013)
Highest degree earned	No	Yes	No	Yes
R-squared	0.140	0.161	0.180	0.209
No. of observations	3,184	3,184	2,712	2,712

NOTES: Standard errors are in parentheses. All models contain controls for demographic, family, and school characteristics. See Table 5.1 for a complete list. If we include the student's college major in addition to his or her GPA and highest degree, the results change minimally. The math effects for males are still measured very imprecisely. For females, the advanced algebra and calculus coefficients drop by about 0.01 and are both significant at the 10 percent level. The other math coefficients change even less. "Yes" indicates whether the specified control variables are in the model.

**Significant at the 5 percent level; *significant at the 10 percent level.

words, we estimate seven new models in which each model interacts the six math curriculum variables with a different school quality measure (student-teacher ratio, percentage of teachers with a master's degree, unionization status of teachers, number of students at the school, length of school year, teacher salary, and school spending). For ethnicity, we estimate just one new model in which all of the ethnic dummy variables in our original model are interacted with each of the math curriculum measures. We also use this latter technique for the models that include interactions with parental income and school rigor.

The following school quality measures did not produce any significant interaction effects: student-teacher ratio, school spending, and number of students in the school. The student characteristics that were not significant were math GPA and parental income when measured in six categories (each of the six income levels interacted with each of the math courses). Most of the interaction terms from the remaining variables were also insignificant.

The overriding conclusion from the interaction analysis is that the predicted effect of math courses does not depend on student or school characteristics. Without taking away from this overall picture, below we briefly discuss the few interaction effects that are statistically significant.[6] In all of these cases, caution should be exercised in interpreting the results. It is important to note that in these new models, many of the direct curriculum effects are no longer statistically significant. The lack of significant interaction terms and the curriculum variables may be the result of collinearity between these covariates. The fact that many of the estimated math effects (both direct and indirect) take on bizarre values in these new models reinforces this assertion.

Table D.2 displays only the significant interaction effects from the series of models that we estimated.[7] Each set of rows represents a separate model in which the particular variable (or set of variables in the case of race, parental income, and school rigor) is interacted with the six math course variables and added to the baseline model that additionally controls for demographic, family, and school characteristics, as well as math GPA and the student's ultimate level of education. For the continuous variables, the top row within any category of school characteristics indicates the predicted effect of a particular mathematics course for students with the average value of the given school

---

[6]Considering that there were 42 potential interaction terms that could be significant (six interaction terms in each of seven school quality models), the fact so few effects were significant reassures us that math curriculum effects are not driven in large part by the school quality measures.

[7]Some insignificant effects are included for expositional purposes.

Table D.2

The Effect of Math Courses on Earnings When the Effect Depends on School or Student Characteristics
(in percent)

	Voc. Math	Pre-Algebra	Algebra/ Geometry	Intermed. Algebra	Advanced Algebra	Calculus
% teachers with a master's						
Math effect at average value			2.74**			
Additional effect for:						
1 standard deviation above			−1.69*			
1 standard deviation below			1.71*			
Teacher salary ($1,000s)						
Math effect at average value		−0.17**				
Additional effect for:						
1 standard deviation above		−1.58**				
1 standard deviation below		1.45**				
% disadvantaged students						
Math effect at average value		0.75*			3.46	
Additional effect for:						
1 standard deviation above		−2.38**			3.09*	
1 standard deviation below		2.07**			−2.56*	
Teacher unionization						
Effect for not unionized			7.66**			−10.13
Additional effect for unionized			−5.57**			16.57*
School rigor						
Effect for low						38.06**
Additional effect for:						
Medium						−33.13*
High						−36.18**
Student's ethnicity						
Math effect for white					1.71	3.36
Additional effect for:						
Black					9.37*	
Hispanic						
Asian						19.15*
Native American						

	Voc. Math	Pre- Algebra	Algebra/ Geometry	Intermed. Algebra	Advanced Algebra	Calculus
Parental income (fewer categories)						
Math effect for lowest		6.88*				
Additional effect for:						
Low income		−6.63				
Medium income		−6.84				
High income		−8.67*				

NOTES: We show additional effects only if significant. For the continuous variables, the top row within any category of school characteristic indicates the predicted effect of a particular mathematics course for students with the average value of the given school characteristic. The next two rows within each category indicate how much that effect changes for students who attend schools with values of the school resource one standard deviation above and below the average value. For the discrete variables, the top row within each student/school characteristic category is the math effect for the stated group of students. The bottom rows represent the change in the math effect experienced by alternative groups of students. The following school qualities and student traits did not have any significant interaction effects: student-teacher ratio, school spending, high school membership, math GPA, and parental income when measured in six categories (each of the six income levels interacted with each of the math courses). The length of the school year interacted with pre-algebra was significant at the 10 percent level; however, it was not economically significant since the effect was so small. The additional effect of math courses given a two standard deviation increase in the school length (six days) was practically zero and so we do not include it in the table. To calculate the additional percentage effects for the discrete variables, we first calculate the math effect for the alternative group as $e^{\beta_1 + \beta_2} - 1$ where β_1 is the coefficient on the math variable and β_2 is the coefficient on the interaction term (the math variable interacted with the discrete variable). From this alternative effect, we subtract the original math effect ($e^{\beta_1} - 1$).

**Significant at the 5 percent level; *significant at the 10 percent level.

characteristics. The next two rows within each category indicate how much that effect changes for students who attend schools with values of the school resource one standard deviation above and below the average value.[8] Similarly, for the discrete variables, the top row within each student/school characteristic category is the math effect for the stated

---

[8]The continuous variables are the percentage of teachers with a master's degree, teacher salary and the percentage of disadvantaged students at the school. The remaining variables take on discrete values.

group of students. The bottom rows represent the change in the math effect experienced by the alternative groups of students.

Teachers with a Master's Degree. There is weak evidence that an increase in the percentage of teachers with a master's degree diminishes the effect of algebra/geometry credits. At an average school where about 49 percent of the teachers hold a master's degree, the predicted effect of an algebra course is 2.74 percent in this model. However, this effect is reduced by 1.69 percentage points for students at schools where the percentage of teachers with a master's degree is 73 (one standard deviation above the average).[9] This does not seem intuitive, but bear in mind that just because there are more teachers at a school with a master's degree, it does not mean that they are necessarily matched to the algebra courses. It is also important to note that the overall effect on earnings from an increase in the percentage of teachers with a master's degree is not negative. Although it is not displayed in the table, the direct effect that increasing the percentage of teachers with a master's degree has on earnings almost completely counterbalances the decrease in the math effect. Therefore, earnings are not predicted to change at all as the result of a more educated group of teachers.

Teacher Salary. Another point of note is the effect of teacher salary on the benefit of pre-algebra courses. At average values of teacher salary, pre-algebra credits are not predicted to have much effect on earnings (−0.17 percent). However, the effect is reduced by 1.58 percentage points at schools where teacher salary is $1,107 (one standard deviation) higher than the average. Such an effect seems counterintuitive, yet we offer one possible explanation. To the extent that lower teacher salary is a proxy for less-affluent schools, this result indicates that an additional course in impoverished areas has more of a "make-or-break" effect on students' life prospects than it would in more affluent areas.

Disadvantaged Students. Increases in the percentage of disadvantaged students at a school appear to cause the lower-level math courses to be less effective and the higher-level courses to be more

---

[9]On the other hand, at schools where only 25 percent of the teachers hold a master's degree (one standard deviation below the average), the predicted effect of algebra increases by 1.71 percentage points.

effective. Thus, students who go to schools with higher shares of disadvantaged students but who take high-level math courses will have a larger increase in earnings from those courses than students at schools with fewer disadvantaged students. If the percentage of disadvantaged students at the school increases by one standard deviation (approximately 25 percentage points), the advanced algebra effect would increase by 3.09 percentage points from 3.46 percent.

Unions. The algebra/geometry math effect may depend somewhat on whether teachers are unionized. In schools where the teachers are not unionized, the predicted effect of an additional algebra/geometry course is 7.66 percent. However, in schools that are unionized, the effect is much smaller at about 2.09 percent.[10] This value is more comparable to the 2.9 percent effect in the baseline model that controls for GPA. Unions themselves may not be the direct cause of this change in effectiveness, because schools may unionize in the presence of larger problems.[11] On the other hand, calculus appears to be more effective in unionized schools. The contrasting effects of unionization are puzzling and a convincing rationalization for them is not forthcoming.

High School Rigor. When we interact high school rigor with math curriculum, we get similar results. To measure a school's rigor, we compute the average highest math level of students attending that school. We then create a three-level variable indicating whether this value is low (less than algebra), medium (algebra or geometry), or high (more than algebra). It turns out that students from schools of the lowest rigor receive a much bigger "kick" from calculus than do students from higher-level schools. At such schools, calculus has a 38 percent predicted effect on earnings. At high-level schools, this effect drops by about 36 percentage points, leaving a 2 percent effect. Getting through calculus at a less-rigorous school (perhaps in the inner city) is a real testament to ability, motivation, and drive and so part of the overall math effect may really be capturing this student characteristic. The models attempt to

---

[10]This is computed by subtracting the additional effect for unionized schools from the effect at non-unionized school.

[11]See Hoxby (1996) for a discussion of the effect of teacher's unions on education production.

mitigate this possibility by controlling for GPA. However, unobserved variations in ability and motivation could still be a part of the explanation.

Ethnicity. There is weak evidence that, relative to white students, black students may benefit more from advanced algebra courses and Asian students from calculus courses.

Parental Income. When we measure parental income in six categories, there is still no evidence of differential math effects. However, if we condense parental income into four categories, there is some weak evidence to indicate that the lowest-income students may benefit more from the lower-level math courses than students from higher-income categories. Yet, once again, we caution that the imprecise nature of the estimates leads to point estimates in which we are not entirely confident.

Do Math Effects Depend on the Student's Educational Attainment?

Following earlier work by Levine and Zimmerman (1995), we considered presenting separate models for subsamples of students based on educational attainment, but we were not confident in the results because of the small sample size of the separate groups.[12] Therefore, we took an alternative approach and estimated interaction models using a strategy similar to that described above. We found very little evidence that the curriculum effects depend on the student's ultimate level of education. In other words, math matters for students of all education levels. This result may be driven by the high amount of correlation among the math variables and the interaction terms.

---

[12]Despite these concerns, we did estimate such models with our data and found that some of the math course coefficients are significant for females with some postsecondary education or with a bachelor's degree, but also for men with a bachelor's degree. The IV results indicate that a couple of the math courses may have effects for a couple of the educational attainment groups, but no clear trends emerge.

Appendix E

Ethnic and Socioeconomic Earnings Gaps, by Gender

In this appendix, we present the regression results from the models that we use to estimate the earnings gaps for students of different ethnic groups and different socioeconomic groups (see Table E.1). In addition, Table E.1 displays models of these earnings gaps broken down by gender.

Table E.1

Earnings Gaps Based on Ethnicity and Parental Income (before and after curriculum is added to the model)

	Pooled				Male		Female	
	(1)	(2)	(3)	(4)	(5)	(6)	(7)	(8)
Native American	-0.229**		-0.102**	-0.068	-0.171**	-0.134**	-0.022	-0.002
	(0.054)		(0.052)	(0.051)	(0.064)	(0.063)	(0.087)	(0.085)
Black	-0.100**		-0.010	-0.0002	-0.094**	-0.081**	0.077**	0.085**
	(0.024)		(0.025)	(0.0249)	(0.033)	(0.032)	(0.039)	(0.039)
Hispanic	-0.052**		0.010	0.036*	-0.042*	-0.019	0.070**	0.103**
	(0.019)		(0.021)	(0.021)	(0.026)	(0.026)	(0.036)	(0.035)
Asian	0.092**		0.072*	0.023	-0.021	-0.056	0.175**	0.109*
	(0.043)		(0.044)	(0.043)	(0.056)	(0.055)	(0.068)	(0.067)
<$7K		-0.293**	-0.171**	-0.124**	-0.157**	-0.121**	-0.200**	-0.133**
		(0.032)	(0.032)	(0.032)	(0.041)	(0.041)	(0.050)	(0.049)
$7K-$15K		-0.098**	-0.039*	-0.025	-0.007	-0.001	-0.066*	-0.041
		(0.023)	(0.022)	(0.022)	(0.028)	(0.028)	(0.034)	(0.034)
$15I-$20K		-0.026	0.002	0.001	0.001	0.034	-0.043	-0.031
		(0.025)	(0.024)	(0.023)	(0.031)	(0.030)	(0.037)	(0.036)
$25K-$38K		0.096**	0.070**	0.070**	0.070**	0.070**	0.076**	0.076**
		(0.026)	(0.025)	(0.025)	(0.032)	(0.031)	(0.040)	(0.039)
$38K +		0.112**	0.058**	0.059**	0.098**	0.099**	0.013	0.018
		(0.030)	(0.029)	(0.029)	(0.036)	(0.035)	(0.048)	(0.047)
Curriculum	No	No	No	Yes	No	Yes	No	Yes
R-squared	0.007	0.035	0.137	0.172	0.103	0.132	0.132	0.155
No. of observations	5,919	5,919	5,919	5,919	3,194	3,194	2,725	2,725

NOTES: Standard errors are in parentheses. The effects of ethnicity are measured relative to whites. The effects of parental income are measured relative to students from families with incomes between $20,000 and $25,000. Each column represents one model. Column 1 contains only ethnicity controls. Column 2 contains only parental income controls. The remaining models control for all of the demographic, family, and school characteristics listed in Table 5.1. The results are effectively the same if we control for math GPA and highest educational degree earned. Within each category (pooled, male, and female), the first column does not control for curriculum whereas the second column does. The change in the effect of any particular variable from the first to the second column represents the portion of the earnings gap that curriculum can explain. "Yes" indicates whether the specified control variables are in the model.

**Significant at the 5 percent level; *significant at the 10 percent level.

142

Bibliography

Altonji, Joseph G. (1995). "The Effects of High School Curriculum on Education and Labor Market Outcomes," *Journal of Human Resources*, 30(3):409–438.

Betts, Julian R. (1998). "The Impact of Educational Standards on the Level and Distribution of Earnings," *American Economic Review*, 88(1):266–275.

Betts, Julian R., Kim Rueben, and Anne Danenberg (2000). *Equal Resources, Equal Outcomes? The Distribution of School Resources and Student Achievement in California*, San Francisco, California: Public Policy Institute of California.

Bishop, Hohn H. (1989). "Why the Apathy in American High Schools?" *Educational Researcher*, 18:6–10, 42.

Blackburn, McKinley L., and David Neumark (1993). "Omitted-Ability Bias and the Increase in Return to Schooling," *Journal of Labor Economics*, 11(3): 521–544.

Costrell, Robert M. (1994). "A Simple Model of Educational Standards," *American Economic Review*, 84(4): 956–971.

Daniel, Kermit, Dan Black, and Jeffrey Smith (1997). "College Quality and the Wages of Young Men," University of Western Ontario, Department of Economics, Research Report 9707, London, Ontario, Canada.

Ehrenberg, Ronald G., and Robert S. Smith (1997). *Modern Labor Economics: Theory and Public Policy*, Reading, Massachusetts: Addison-Wesley.

Gamoran, Adam (1998). "The Impact of Academic Course Work on Labor Market Outcomes for Youth Who Do Not Attend College: A Research Review," in Adam Gamoran and Harold Himmelfarb (eds.), *The Quality of Vocational Education: Background Paper from the 1994 National Assessment of Vocational Education,* Washington, D.C.: National Institute on Postsecondary Education, Libraries, and Lifelong Learning, Office of Educational Research and Improvement, U.S. Department of Education.

Griliches, Zvi (1977). "Estimating the Returns to Schooling: Some Econometric Problems," *Econometrica*, 45(1):1–22.

Greene, William H. (1993). *Econometric Analysis*, New York: Macmillan Publishing Company.

Grogger, Jeff, and Eric Eide (1995). "Changes in College Skills and the Rise in the College Wage Premium," *Journal of Human Resources*, 30(2):280–310.

Grogger, Jeff (1996). "School Expenditures and Post-Schooling Earnings: Evidence from High School and Beyond," *The Review of Economics and Statistics*, 78(4):628–637.

Hoxby, Caroline Minter (1996). "How Teacher's Unions Affect Education Production," *Quarterly Journal of Economics,* 111(3):671–718.

Ingels, Steven, et al. (1995). *National Longitudinal Study of 1988—Second Follow-Up: Transcript Component Data File User's Manual,* Washington, D.C.: National Center for Education Statistics (NCES 94-377).

James, Estelle, Nabeel Alsalam, Joseph C. Conaty, and Duc-le To (1989). "College Quality and Future Earnings: Where Should You Send Your Child to College?" *American Economic Review* (May):247–252.

Jones, Calvin, et al. (1982). *High School and Beyond: Transcripts Survey: Data File User's Manual,* Washington, D.C.: National Center for Education Statistics.

Levine, Phillip B., and David J. Zimmerman (1995). "The Benefit of Additional High-School Math and Science Classes for Young Men and Women," *Journal of Business & Economic Statistics,* 13(2):137–149.

Lillard, Dean R. (1998). "Accounting for Substitution Between Credentials in Estimates of the Returns to GED and High School Diplomas," unpublished manuscript, Ithaca, New York: Cornell University.

Manski, Charles F., and David A. Wise, with contributions by Winship C. Fuller and Steven F. Venti (1983). *College Choice in America,* Cambridge, Massachusetts: Harvard University Press.

Morgan, James N., and Greg J. Duncan (1979). "College Quality and Earnings," *Research in Human Capital and Development,* (1):103–121.

Murnane, Richard J., John B. Willett, and Frank Levy (1995). "The Growing Importance of Cognitive Skills in Wage Determination," *The Review of Economics and Statistics,* 77(2):251–266.

Porter, A. C., M. W. Kirst, E. J. Osthoff, J. S. Smithson, and S. A. Schneider (1993). *Reform Up Close: An Analysis of High School Mathematics and Science Classrooms,* Consortium for Policy Research in Education Final Report, Madison, Wisconsin: University of Wisconsin-Madison, Wisconsin Center for Education Research.

Reed, Deborah (1999). *California's Rising Income Inequality: Causes and Concerns,* San Francisco, California: Public Policy Institute of California.

Rumberger, Russell W., and Scott L. Thomas (1993). "The Economic Returns to College Major, Quality and Performance: A Multilevel

Analysis of Recent Graduates," *Economics of Education Review*, 12(1):1–19.

Spence, Michael (1973). "Job Market Signalling," *Quarterly Journal of Economics*, 87(3):355–374.

About the Authors

HEATHER ROSE

Heather Rose is a research fellow at the Public Policy Institute of California, specializing in the economics of education. Her research interests also include school finance and how different racial groups are affected by the educational process. Her current projects include a study of affirmative action policies at the college level and a study of how high school curriculum affects the test score gap between white and minority students. She holds a B.A. in economics from the University of California, Berkeley, and an M.A. and Ph.D. in economics from the University of California, San Diego.

JULIAN R. BETTS

Julian Betts is a senior fellow at the Public Policy Institute of California and an associate professor of economics at the University of California, San Diego. Much of his research over the past decade has focused on the economic analysis of public schools. He has written extensively on the link between student outcomes and measures of school spending, including class size, teachers' salaries, and teachers' level of education. More recently, he has examined the role that standards and expectations play in student achievement. His other main areas of research include higher education; immigration; technology, skills, and the labor market; and the economics of unions. He holds an M.Phil. in economics from Oxford University, England, and a Ph.D. in economics from Queen's University, Kingston, Ontario, Canada.

Other Related PPIC Publications

The Changing Role of Education in the California Labor Market
Julian R. Betts

Equal Resources, Equal Outcomes? The Distribution of School Resources and Student Achievement in California
Julian R. Betts, Kim S. Rueben, Anne Danenberg

For Better or For Worse? School Finance Reform in California
Jon Sonstelie, Eric Brunner, Kenneth Ardon

School Finance and California's Master Plan for Education
Jon Sonstelie, Peter Richardson (editors)

PPIC publications may be ordered by phone or from our website
(800) 232-5343 [mainland U.S.]
(415) 291-4400 [Canada, Hawaii, overseas]
www.ppic.org